First Steps:
A comprehensive guide to financial Matters after a death

Shane Phillips
First Step Solutions, LLC

www.FirstStepsHelp.com
info@FirstStepsHelp.com

Back Cover Photo of Shane Phillips courtesy of:
Brad Mikel
Mikel Gamber Photography
www.mikel-gamber.com

First Edition: April 2013
Printed in the United States of America
ISBN: 978-0615802718

Disclaimer

Acknowledgements

I owe a deep debt of gratitude to my wife Valerie for her encouragement to write this book. Without her unwavering support this book would not have been possible. Thank you Valerie, for giving me the time away from family responsibilities to make this happen. I am thankful for my children's curiosity and enthusiasm as I embarked on this endeavor. Thank you Andrew, Annalisa, Aidan, Audrey, and Gus!

So many people have influenced me professionally and personally. Without their lasting impact on my life, this book would not have happened. I am thankful to Phil Beeson, Wil Armstrong, Steve Sittko, John Horan, Jennifer McBride, Mary Lyles, Anne & Kelly Kramer, Art & Kathy Phillips, and my late grandmother Wanda Phillips. Each of you has helped me in so many ways.

I am also very thankful to Christa Wickland and Coralie Strasenburgh for their editorial assistance. As well as Scott and & Maura Spangler for assistance with the insurance chapter, and Kerri Klein for help with the Probate and Estate chapter.

Dedication

This book is dedicated to my late parents Alvin and Judy Phillips, my sister Mindy, and my cousin Adrian. I miss each of you dearly. As painful as it was to lose you, your passing and my resulting experiences were the inspiration for this book.

Table of Contents

Preface: My Journey

The Island of Corsica is located west of Italy and south of France, in the Mediterranean Sea. Corsica is one of the 27 regions (or states) of France. With its tropic-like climate, beautiful beaches, and French-Italian culture, it is a favored vacation destination for many Europeans. Corsica is the birthplace of French Emperor Napoleon Bonaparte and Explorer Christopher Columbus. In 1989, Corsica also became the place where my life changed forever.

I grew up in the Washington D.C. area. My parents owned a small computer consulting business in McLean, Virginia. My parents had a passion for travel, learning, and exposing my sister Mindy and me to new opportunities. When I was young, we had a string of foreign exchange students live with us. We traveled to Europe as a family when Mindy and I were just 4 and 6 years old. As we got older, my parents set the expectation that both of us would become exchange students at some point during high school.

When I reached my freshman year in high school, my parents decided that I should go to Germany as an exchange student. I had mixed feelings about leaving home for nearly a year. I really enjoyed my school and friends. I did not want to miss a year of playing football and all the other fun parts of being an American teenage boy. But my parents were insistent that I have the experience of studying abroad. So, I reluctantly began taking German language classes. What I did not know at the time was that this very decision to travel abroad would ultimately save my life.

My father did some consulting work with the German military attaché to the United States, Colonel Hans Sieber. Col. Sieber had a friend named Klaus Vorrink in Germany who wanted to send his daughter, Nicole, to the United States for a year to study English. A private exchange was arranged between the two families; I was to go to Germany to live with the Vorrinks, while Nicole was to come to the United States to live with my family.

The Vorrink's invited me to travel to Germany several weeks before school actually started. They had planned a vacation to Italy, France, and Corsica and wanted me to go with them. On July 5, 1989 I left my family and flew to Germany, ready to embark on my European adventure.

I arrived in Germany to a very warm welcome by the Vorrink family and their friends. The Vorrink's lived in the little town of Neuenhaus (population 9,600) located in the northwest corner of Germany. They had a big arrival party and made me feel very welcome in their home.

About two weeks after I arrived in Germany, we set out on our vacation to Corsica. My host mother Helga, and her daughter Nicole and I, drove south through Germany. We toured several cities in Germany, and then went on to Lake Como and Florence, Italy. Klaus, and their other daughter Katrina, flew to Nice, France where the Vorrinks kept their boat. The plan was for Klaus and Katrina to sail their boat to Corsica and meet up with Helga, Nicole and myself.

After our tour of Germany, Switzerland, and Italy, Helga, Nicole and I boarded a ferry ship to Corsica. After a four hour ride from Livorno, Italy to Bastia, Corsica we met up with Klaus and Katrina. It was Thursday, July 27, 1989. I remember the date vividly because it was the last time I ever spoke with my parents and sister. I called my parents every few days to check in. On this day when I called, I was able to reach my mom at my parent's office. They had just recently purchased a multi-line phone system, so she wanted to see if she could patch my dad and sister into the call. She reached my sister at home and my dad in his car (cell phones and conference calling were a novelty back then). I honestly don't remember much of what we talked about, just that we were in four different places, together again as a family...

The next few days on Corsica were fun, but uneventful. We did some snorkeling and generally relaxed. We sailed the boat around the perimeter of Corsica, going from the port city of Bastia to Ajaccio. When we got to Ajaccio, we anchored in the harbor, registered our boat at the marina and went out to dinner.

The next morning, August 2, 1989, two Ajaccio Harbor Police Officers approached our boat. They spoke only French. Klaus and his family spoke German and I spoke English. The police had an urgent message for an American boy name John Philip. The officer said "John Philip call home!" We deduced that that the message was for me. I then went to a pay phone at the Harbor Police Office.

First, I tried calling our home in Virginia. But there was no answer. Then, I tried calling my parent's office. No Answer. It was the middle of the night in the United States. I was getting worried that something had happened. My next thought was to call my best friend from high school, Elvis Oxley. His mother answered the phone. She told me that it was important I reach someone in my family, but she could not tell me what had happened.

Perplexed, I finally called my grandmother in Colorado, Wanda Phillips. Despite the fact that it was 3 a.m. in Denver, she answered. "Grandma," I said, "what's going on? I can't reach my parents anywhere, and I have an urgent message to call home!" Her response to me was, "Shaney, you don't know yet, do you?" There was a long pause on the other end of the phone and I said, "Know what, Grandma?" I can still hear her words clearly, "Your Mommy, Daddy, and Mindy were killed in a plane crash!"

I sunk to the floor not comprehending what I had just heard. How? Why?

A few years prior to the accident, my father had bought into an airplane partnership. He had been a pilot since he was 17 years old. Owning a plane had been a dream of his. As his small consulting business grew, he was able to save the money necessary to buy into the partnership. As a family, we enjoyed trips to the beach and other destinations up and down the east coast.

This trip began as many of our trips did, with an impulse to go somewhere. It was a hot summer day in Virginia. My parents decided that they would take my sister and her friend Mandy Hope to the beach in Atlantic City, New Jersey, for the day. The outbound trip was uneventful. They spent time on the beach, had dinner, and then departed Atlantic City for Manassas, Virginia. As they approached Virginia, the weather changed significantly. According to the National Transportation Safety Board report, there was a severe thunderhead. The investigators suspected that my dad succumbed to vertigo, a spatial disorientation affliction that can cause pilots to lose their bearing. As a result, he essentially drove the plane into the ground.

Through sobs and tears, I told Klaus and Helga the horrible news about my family. Klaus immediately began making plans to get me back to the United States. He graciously insisted on traveling with me all the way home. He and I traveled together from Corsica, to Paris, to Frankfurt, and then ultimately to Washington D.C.

The trip back to the United States took over a day. I don't remember much about it. I was numb with fear, disbelief, and grief. But the thought that kept resonating in my head was: "Everything is different now…."

In a split second, my life had changed. My life went from being a part of a closely-knit family of four, to being an orphan at the age of sixteen. From privilege and opportunity, to fear and grief. Everything was different now.

We arrived at Dulles International Airport in Virginia to a throng of reporters, T.V. crews, friends and most importantly, my German Shepard, Kessi. Local television news stations, as well as the *Washington Post* and *Washington Times*, extensively covered the plane crash. The story stayed in the headlines for several days.

The day after my arrival in Virginia, Klaus and I flew to Denver, Colorado. My family was originally from Colorado and most of my extended family lived there. My family collectively decided that my parents and sister would be buried in Denver. The funeral occurred on a bright Saturday morning. So many people attended the service; it had to be held outside, with space expanded to include standing room in the parking lot.

After the funeral services, I remained in Denver for a few days and tried to figure out what to do. Klaus graciously offered for me to return to Germany. My maternal grandparents "insisted" that I would be moving to their tiny town in the mountains of Colorado. Others opened their homes to me back in Virginia. Ultimately, I decided to return to Virginia and go back to my high school.

I lived with a well-meaning family for a couple of months but, it was not a good fit for me or for them. So, Kessi and I went back to our house (which was for sale at this point), and tried to live in the house on our own. But, when you are sixteen there a lot of things you don't think through, like where you will get money, food, etc. So, we only lasted on our own for a few days.

There was a young couple named Phil and Jory Beeson that lived a few houses down from me. I had done some animal sitting for them in the past. Along with their one-year-old daughter Rebecca, Phil and Jory shared the home with Jory's parents. I really didn't know them that well, but they had always been very kind to me. So, with my options reduced to staying in my house until it sold, going back to Colorado, or finding someplace else to live, I went with option number three and decided to try to find someplace else to live.

I knocked on the Beesons' door and asked if I could sleep on their couch. They welcomed me in with open arms. After a few days as a guest, I asked if I could stay with them permanently. They agreed and I began the process of moving in with them.

My father was 39 and my mother was 40 when they died. They had given no thought to an estate plan, or a plan for how my sister and I would be cared for in the event of their untimely passing, nor did they have any life insurance. This lack of planning left me in a very bad spot. The business they owned was not sustainable without my parent's involvement. They had a lot of debt and few assets that could be liquidated to help cover the debts of the estate.

I believe God had a plan for me. When I was at the lowest of all possible lows- orphaned, significant estate debt, and no means of support God saved me from what was otherwise a hopeless situation. Phil and Jory were both attorneys. Phil was also a CPA. With help from them both, I was able to work through the challenges I faced.

Jory had worked in child protective services for part of her career. She understood how the system worked. With the help of some other attorneys, she was able to have me emancipated as a minor. This enabled me to avoid becoming a part of the social services labyrinth. Phil worked with my parent's business attorney to resolve much of the estate liabilities. They also collaborated on the sale of the business to the company's employees. And, Phil helped with the sale of my house.

While all of this was going on I was also trying to come to terms with my grief and the loss of my family. About 6 months after the accident, I met a young man a few years older than me by the name of Wil Armstrong. Wil was a graduate of my high school, and had just recently graduated from college. He knew of me because his first job was at the bank where my parents had done their business banking. He was also one of the local leaders of Young Life in our town. Young Life is a youth oriented, non-denominational, out-reach ministry. Through Wil and Young Life, I accepted Jesus Christ as my savior. This was a critical step to my healing. Young Life provided me with a sense of family and also helped me comprehend my loss from a spiritual perspective.

I went on to graduate from Langley High School in 1991. After being away from my extended family, I was ready to return to my roots. I decided to attend college in my home state of Colorado. I was accepted at the University of Denver and began my freshman year at DU in the fall of 1991.

Through the generosity of friends, neighbors, and people I did not even know, some money was raised to help me pay for my college tuition. I paid for the rest of my education via grants and loans.

About the time that I moved to Colorado, Wil and his family also returned to Colorado. Wil's father, Bill Armstrong, had represented Colorado in both the 5th Congressional district and as a two term U. S. Senator from Colorado. The Armstrong's purchased a small mortgage banking firm in Colorado called Cherry Creek Mortgage Company. While I was at DU, the Armstrong's offered me an internship at CCMC, so I could learn the basics of residential finance. This was my start in financial services.

I went on to graduate from DU and to work for Cherry Creek Mortgage Company for several years, before transitioning to the wealth management profession in 2008. Today, I serve as Director of Wealth Management for Wakefield Asset Management, a Colorado based wealth management firm. I met my wife, Valerie, in 1999. We were married in 2000, and are the proud parents of five wonderful children: Andrew, Annalisa, Aidan, Audrey, and August.

In 2003, I read the book, "The Purpose Driven Life," by Pastor Rick Warren. The first chapter of this book is essentially about the fact that your life is not about you, rather it's about your purpose for being here. As I paused to reflect on my life and purpose, some things came into perspective for me. My life was about more than just being a husband, father, and breadwinner. It was about leaving a positive and indelible mark on my community.

One of the things I had greatly struggled with was not ever having had any professional grief counseling. Phil and Jory had tried to encourage me to see a counselor, but that was short lived. Not because of a lack of effort on their part, but because I scoffed at the idea. In retrospect, I wish that I had dealt with my grief and feelings earlier on. Now that I was a parent, I trembled at the thought of how young I was when my parents and sister died. I wanted to help other children who were facing the challenges one faces after the loss of a parent.

So, I set out to create a non-profit counseling service that would provide grief counseling to Denver area children after a loss. I partnered with Dr. Mary Lyles who specialized in children's grief and counseling. Together, we created The Children's Grief Education Association (CGEA) in 2004.

Over a six-year period, we were able to serve more than 400 Denver area children that had suffered a loss. Due to family circumstances, Mary had to relocate to the Houston area in 2010, where she continues her work in private practice. I merged the assets of CGEA into a larger organization called HeartLight Center (www.HeartLightCenter.org).

HeartLight Center is a not-for-profit organization founded by John Horan and Jennifer McBride of Horan McConaty Funeral Homes. HeartLight Center provides affordable grief support and education for adults and children in the Denver community who are experiencing grief associated with death and loss.

Much of my work at HeartLight Center has been focused on working with the Widows and Widowers Group. Through both my volunteer work with the Widows and Widowers Group at

HeartLight, and my professional work as a Wealth Manager it became very apparent to me that there are a number of complicated issues surrounding grief and loss as it relates to finances, investments, and banking. Very few people are equipped to work through these issues and even fewer know where to start.

This book is the culmination of my professional experience and community service, coupled with my life experiences with grief and loss. It is my hope this book will provide the reader with a road map for addressing financial issues for those who are grieving.

Introduction

If you are reading this book, you have likely experienced some significant changes in your life in the past few days, weeks, or months. Perhaps you have lost a spouse, parent, a sibling, child, or other family member. Regardless of whom you have lost, or how you came to read this book, please know your loss and grief is unique to you and your situation.

The purpose of this workbook is to provide you with the information and tools you will need for handling financial matters after the death of a person in your life. I wrote this book because I have been in your shoes, or a pair of shoes very similar to the ones you are wearing right now. I have also spent virtually my entire professional career in financial services, and have devoted much of my free time to several non-profit organizations that focus on helping people work through grief issues related to death.

This workbook is divided into two parts: First Steps and Notifications.

> **Part I: First Steps** - addresses immediate needs, document gathering, estate issues, and the hiring of professional advisors to assist you.
>
> **Part II: Notifications** - examines how to obtain benefits, notification of employers and other groups, identity protection for the deceased, making life insurance claims, closing/transferring bank and investment accounts, how to handle estate debt, and closing email and social media accounts.

At the end of each chapter is a section for creating your own action item checklist. Each chapter also has a page for taking notes. Finally, in the Appendix section there are some useful state-specific internet links and sample forms.

It is my sincere hope you find this book useful. Most of all, I hope the information shared helps to ease your burden. There is no magic potion, formula, or spell that will make you feel better. Time and remembrance are the best elixirs to the pain of grief.

Thank you for taking the time to read this book and invest in your own future!

Warm regards,

Shane E. Phillips
America's End - Of - Life Financial Expert TM

Part I: First Steps

Part I, addresses the First Steps that need to be taken, regardless of who has passed away. This section is divided into four chapters. Each chapter addresses a unique concept.

Chapter 1: Immediate Needs

This chapter deals with how to seek help from friends and family, how to make funeral arrangements, how to write obituary, and obtaining a death certificate.

Chapter 2: Document Gathering

There are a number of documents you will need to gather for the tasks that must be addressed in the coming days. This chapter explains which documents you will need and their purpose.

Chapter 3 Estates, Wills, & Probate

Estate law, wills, and the probate process are not things most people deal with on a regular basis. This chapter is a basic primer for understanding some of the legal issues you may encounter.

Chapter 4: Hiring Professional Advisors

Depending on your situation, you may need to hire professional advisors such as an estate/probate attorney, financial adviser, or accountant. This chapter will help you understand what to look for when hiring professionals

Chapter 1: Immediate Needs

There are a number of tasks you will need to complete over the course of the next few days, weeks, and months. Some of these tasks will be easier than others. There may be moments that are very difficult. Reminders of the deceased person will undoubtedly occur on occasion, as you complete these tasks. You might feel angry that he did not do a better job of planning for his own death, or was not as organized as you would have liked him to have been.

It is okay to feel this way. You will have good days and bad days. Some issues will be easier to resolve than others. The good news is you will make it through this. There is light at the end of the tunnel. In this chapter, we will look at some of the first things that need to be addressed when a person passes away. You may have purchased or received this book weeks or months after your loss, so, some of these first steps may already have been handled.

Support from friends and family

It is strongly recommended that you find an individual, or a group of friends and family, who you can count on to help you through the coming days. There is strength in numbers. If you can obtain the assistance of a few trustworthy family members or friends, it will pay dividends in the future.

Likely, you have already heard from friends who have said, "Let me know what I can do to help." People genuinely mean this when they say it. The problem is, so few people know what to do or how to be helpful. Often the inclination is to offer to provide a meal. Those offers are well meaning and made with good intentions.

There will be a number of things that you will need to take care of in order to settle the estate and resolve outstanding financial matters. When you try to do this along with coping with your own grief, it can be an overwhelming and exhausting process. Having a friend to help you with the details, and help you remember what needs to be done, can be very helpful. Seek help from family members, friends, and spiritual leaders you trust.

In addition to planning the funeral or memorial service there are a few things you might need immediate help with, including:

- Answering the phone
- Mail collection
- Care for pets
- Meals
- Cleaning out perishable food / trash removal at decedent's home

While seeking the assistance of others is encouraged, be wary of people that pop up and are too helpful - especially financial, legal, or insurance advisors with whom neither you nor your family have had a previous relationship. If you do not have a financial advisor of some sort, you will need to obtain referrals from friends or family that you trust. Hiring advisors to assist you will be covered more extensively in Chapter 4.

It is wise to talk with a grief counselor, therapist, or spiritual advisor. Whether you are a man or woman, young or in the twilight of your life, talking with a professional that is trained in grief counseling is strongly encouraged. Everyone grieves differently. Talking with a professional about your feelings, fears, or anxieties as the result of your loss can be very beneficial.

Funeral Arrangements

Once you have notified family and friends, you will need to start making funeral arrangements. If the deceased was your spouse, you may already know what her wishes were in terms of funeral arrangements. If you are not aware of final arrangement plans, then you will want to start by looking through the decedent's personal papers or safety deposit box (if you have access). Look for a prepaid burial plan, a membership in a memorial society, or other written instruction regarding her funeral plans. If you are unable to locate any pre-planning documents or other written instructions, you will need to start the funeral planning process.

Planning a funeral or memorial service, is something for which few are prepared. But, this is a time to honor the person who has died and to celebrate her life. The process of planning a service may be difficult, but you may also find moments of joy as you do one last thing for the deceased. Taking a trusted friend or family member with you to the funeral home will make the process easier. Having a third party can also be helpful as you make decisions about the service.

~Tips~

- **Take a trusted friend or family member to help with arrangements.**
- **It is your right to compare funeral costs.**
- **If the deceased was a veteran, you may be entitled to free services from the VA**

Burial assistance may be available from your county if the decedent was on public assistance. You will want to contact the County Department of Social Services to find out if your situation qualifies for assistance. County assistance is limited in terms of total expenses covered. If you think the decedent may qualify for assistance, you will want to contact the county prior to contacting a funeral home.

As with all businesses, there are many types of funeral homes. Some funeral homes work by referral. Others advertise in the yellow pages, online, and on billboards. Some families have used the same funeral home for generations. Regardless of how you choose the funeral home that will care for the deceased, there are a few things of which you need to be aware: Funeral prices vary greatly. It is important to consider cost when making a decision. It is okay to price shop by phone prior to meeting with a funeral director. In many states, funeral homes are required by law to give you an estimate without obligation (similar to a Good Faith Estimate for a home mortgage).

If the decedent served in the military, and was discharged in good standing, he is entitled to a variety of benefits from the Veterans Administration.

Veteran's benefits can include:

- Burial and a grave marker in a national cemetery for the veteran, spouse, and dependent children
- Playing of "Taps"
- Folding and presentation of the American Flag

For deaths of active duty personnel and retirees the following benefits may be available:

- Honor Guard and 21-gun salute
- Burial at sea
- Presidential Memorial Certificate
- Burial / funeral-expense allowance

The staff at your funeral home should be able to help you with these arrangements. You may also contact Veterans Affairs toll free at 1-800-827-1000, or by going to their website, http://www.cem.va.gov/.

Finally, a person may have written instructions as to what should happen with their remains and what ceremonies are to be held. In some states, those instructions legally must be followed. For example, in the author's home state of Colorado, this document is called a Declaration of Disposition of Last Remains. It is a legally enforceable document.

Paying for the funeral

As mentioned above, funerals can vary greatly in price. Most funeral homes will want a deposit up front to cover the cost of caring for the deceased. The balance of the payment will be due when services are completed. There are several ways to pay for the services including cash, credit card, funeral home financing, or a life insurance benefit advance.

A life insurance benefit advance is a loan against the payout from a life insurance policy. If you do not have access to cash or credit to pay for the funeral services, you might consider this option. Funeral costs can also be reimbursed by the estate as a "priority claim". So, you may pay these out of your own funds and then seek to have the estate pay you back. Regardless of how you end up paying for the service, make sure you clearly understand the terms and any financing charges. If things are not clear, it is your right to stop the process and seek further information.

Writing an Obituary or Eulogy

It has become increasingly popular to honor a deceased person with a detailed obituary and then post that obituary online. While writing an obituary is a great way to pay tribute to someone, posting a detailed copy of that obituary online could prove to be hazardous!

The stealing of deceased persons' identities is one of the fastest growing forms of identity theft in America. With the availability of so much personal information on the internet, it is not difficult for a criminal to combine publicly available information with information from an obituary and have enough data to steal a person's identity.

When writing an obituary that will be publicly available in print or on-line, heed the following points:

- Birth date and death date: Use the year only, not the specific month and day

- Do not include the decedent's mother's maiden name, as this is often used as a security question by financial institutions

- Limit information on occupation and address, as this can be used to open new credit accounts or driver's licenses

~Tips~

If you need tips or help writing an obituary or eulogy there are several online sources that can be of assistance. These websites will provide you with information on how to structure an obituary or eulogy. They also provide helpful content such as famous quotes that you might want to include in the eulogy:

www.obituaryguide.com
www.remembranceprocess.com
www.obituarieshelp.org

Funeral directors can also be a great resource in assisting with writing obituaries.

Obtaining a Death Certificate

When a person passes away, a death certificate is issued to certify the death. Unless the death occurs outside the United States, the certificate is issued by the state in which the person died. Death certificates serve three primary purposes:

1. To indicate the cause of death
2. Required in order to conduct a burial, cremation, organ donation, or to transport the deceased across state lines.
3. Required in order to make claim to a person's life insurance or other assets.

Before a death certificate is issued, authorities will require a certification from a coroner, medical examiner, or physician that indicates the identity and cause of death of the deceased. Depending on how, where, and under what circumstances the person died, the death certificate may take several days to obtain. For example, if a person passed away in a hospital, had a long-term illness, and a physician attended the death, then the certification from the physician should be fairly quick and easy to obtain. If, however, the person died alone or under questionable circumstances, then it may take the coroner or medical examiner several days to determine the cause of death and issue the death certificate. Sometimes, a temporary death certificate is issued until the medical tests are completed and the cause of death be certified.

Each state and legal jurisdiction has its own rules for who may sign a death certificate. You may want to consult your state's vital records division or your state medical examiner or county coroner if you need more specific information for your situation. The Appendix at the back of this books lists contact information for the vital statistics office of each state.

Often, a funeral home can be of assistance in obtaining certified copies of the death certificate.. Funeral homes have the expertise and experience to efficiently obtain the certificate. You will want to request 10-15 legal certified death certificates, as you will likely need multiple original certificates when dealing with banks, insurance copies, and other entities.

Chapter Summary

Seek help: People want to be helpful when a person passes away. Often they don't know how to be helpful. Find someone that you trust, and let him help you with the many tasks that lie ahead.

Funeral Arrangements: Bring family members and any close friends who will be involved in the services or who you think could be helpful.

Writing an Obituary: In a time of rampant identity theft, it is important to limit the amount of personal information included in published obituaries.

Death Certificate: You will need to obtain a death certificate in order to bury the deceased. You will also need several original or certified copies of the Certificate in order to settle the estate and financial matters. The funeral home should be able to help you with obtaining the certified copies of the death certificate.

☑ ***Action Steps***

- ☐ ______________________________
- ☐ ______________________________
- ☐ ______________________________
- ☐ ______________________________
- ☐ ______________________________
- ☐ ______________________________
- ☐ ______________________________
- ☐ ______________________________
- ☐ ______________________________
- ☐ ______________________________
- ☐ ______________________________
- ☐ ______________________________
- ☐ ______________________________
- ☐ ______________________________
- ☐ ______________________________
- ☐ ______________________________
- ☐ ______________________________
- ☐ ______________________________
- ☐ ______________________________
- ☐ ______________________________

My Notes

Chapter 2: Understanding Estates, Wills, and Probate

With the funeral completed, it is now time to turn your attention to financial and legal matters. People often don't know where to start when it comes to understanding an estate, a will, and the probate process. This chapter will familiarize you with these terms and provide an overview of the process. There are thousands of books written about estates and wills. And, there is an entire subspecialty within the law known as Estate and Probate law dedicated exclusively to the process of creating estate plans and distributing assets upon death. This chapter is not a substitute for seeking qualified legal counsel for your particular situation, rather it is simply a road map to help you get the process started. It is also important to note that Estate Law is different in each state. Therefore, it is recommended that you seek information about the statutes in your state. If you need help understanding your states laws, please refer to the Appendix of this book. There you will find internet links and phone numbers for the Bar Association in your state.

What is an estate?

An estate includes all of the assets of the deceased, such as real estate, personal property, accounts, investments, automobiles, etc.

What is a will?

A will is a legal *declaration* authored by a living person that states how he wants his assets distributed upon death.

What is probate?

The word "probate" is commonly used to refer to the administration of a deceased person's estate. After death, an estate is either viewed "testate" or "intestate."

- **Testate**: A person has died with a valid will and therefore the assets of the estate are distributed in accordance with the will.

- **Intestate**: A person has died without a valid will and therefore the assets are distributed in accordance with the provisions of state law, or intestate succession.

Locating the will

Locating the will is an important first step in starting the process of distributing assets. Most often you will find the will in the decedent's home. If it is not in her home, it may be in a safe deposit box, at an attorney's office, or pre-registered with the district court. When the original signed will is found, register it with the probate court in the county where the deceased lived. If a will cannot be found, an attorney can help guide you through the intestate probate process. Also, look for a handwritten list of instructions, a letter to family or other similar documents. Depending on the state, these documents may stand in place of a will.

What if the will is in a safe deposit box?

Any person whose name is associated with the box may access a safe deposit box. In addition, an heir or beneficiary named in a will can ask the bank to search the box for the will, burial instructions, or the deed to a burial plot. The bank will open the box in the presence of the heir or beneficiary and remove what is in the box. If a will is located in the safety deposit box, it is the bank's responsibility to deliver the will to the court. You may also want to ask the bank to make you a copy of the will. After the will is filed with the court, the personal representative named in the will can file a petition or application with the court to appoint her or him.

Personal Representative

If you are nominated as personal representative in a will, you have the power, before the court appoints you, to carry out written instructions of the deceased relating to the body, funeral and burial arrangements. You may also begin to protect and safeguard the deceased's assets. Do not remove or distribute assets before opening the estate. The personal representative is the court representative who has the authority to search for any important documents. The search should include the home, office, place of business, and any safe deposit boxes. It is advised to meet with advisors such as accountants, investment professionals, insurance agents, and attorneys. Any information indicating that an asset exists or that bills are unpaid should be kept for use in the administration of the estate.

<u>If you were the deceased person's power of attorney or guardian, your authority to act on that person's behalf ends at death</u> (unless the person was a minor). You will not be able to use these documents to handle the estate.

How are assets distributed?

Many people assume that a will controls the distribution of all assets at the time of death. In reality, asset distribution is controlled in four distinct ways at the time of death:

1. Joint Ownership
2. Beneficiary Designations
3. Trust Distribution
4. Probate Distributions

Below is an overview of each of these categories which will give you a better understanding of how certain assets might be handled:

<u>Joint ownership</u>

The most common way assets are passed at death is by joint ownership. There are two common types of joint ownership:

1. **Tenancy by the Entirety**: This is a form of joint ownership between husband and wife.

2. **Joint Tenancy with Right of Survivorship**. This is a form of joint ownership that may exist between anyone, including multiple individuals.

Beneficiary Designation

Life insurance, annuities, and retirement accounts are typically all directed by beneficiary designations. This means that the deceased person pre-assigned who would receive the assets upon death. These assets are not directed by a will, unless the estate has been named as the beneficiary. If no beneficiary is named, or survives, and the policy or contract does not provide default beneficiaries, then the will or probate court will determine the disposition of the asset.

Trust Distribution

Assets that are owned by, or are payable to, a trust are distributed at death as provided under the terms of the trust. They are not distributed according to a will.

Probate Distribution

Assets which are not payable to joint owners, by beneficiary designation, or through a trust, are distributed through probate at death. Each state has it's own set of probate laws that govern how probate is handled. Sixteen States have adopted the Uniform Probate Code, which prescribes a set way to handle probate cases. Other states have adopted portions of the uniform code. Contact information for each state's Bar Association is provided in the Appendix. Please contact your states association for more information on how probate is handled in your state.

Probate distribution or administration may not be necessary upon the death of an individual. If the person owned no assets titled in his name alone, then there no assets to transfer, and no need for probate. For example, if spouses own all of their property together as husband and wife, then upon the death of the first spouse, the property passes automatically to the surviving spouse without the need for probate. Also, if the deceased made a trust, which contained all of her assets, probate will not be necessary.

Probate is generally handled at the district court level in a special court called a probate court. This may vary state to state, so you will want to check with the county in which the deceased resided to confirm the jurisdiction of the probate court. The probate process is public. This means that the decedent's will becomes a public document when it is filed with the court. You may also have to fill out a statement indicating all of the assets the person owned. This, too, may become a public record. Probate times will vary by jurisdiction, but generally speaking, the process will take about six months. The costs associated with probate generally relate to the professionals you hire to assist with the process. This may include an attorney, financial advisor, CPA, realtor, or other financial professional. There may also be nominal court fees.

Tax Considerations

Depending on the size of the estate, there may be tax considerations for both the estate and those that inherit any assets. The type of asset, value, and inheritor's relationship to the deceased are important factors in determining whether or not taxes need to be paid. Individuals that inherit assets are strongly encouraged to consult with a Certified Public Accountant to determine what tax liability may exist. Please see Chapter 4 for specific questions to ask when hiring a CPA/Accountant. The Appendix of this book also contains a state specific CPA Society contact list.

Chapter Summary

***Locate the will*:** If a will exists, locating an original signed copy will help speed the distribution of assets.

***Personal Representative*:** The will appoints a personal representative. If not, one will need to be appointed before any assets can be distributed.

***Seek Professional Guidance*:** If the estate is complex or you don't clearly understand how the estate will be viewed by a probate court, seek professional guidance from an attorney that specializes in probate matters.

***Be mindful of tax consequences*:** Before distributing any assets to heirs, review the tax consequences. Heirs and other beneficiaries may be required to pay federal and state taxes on assets received.

☑ ***Action Steps***

- ☐ ____________________
- ☐ ____________________
- ☐ ____________________
- ☐ ____________________
- ☐ ____________________
- ☐ ____________________
- ☐ ____________________
- ☐ ____________________
- ☐ ____________________
- ☐ ____________________
- ☐ ____________________
- ☐ ____________________
- ☐ ____________________
- ☐ ____________________
- ☐ ____________________
- ☐ ____________________
- ☐ ____________________
- ☐ ____________________
- ☐ ____________________

My Notes

Chapter 3: Document Gathering

Now that you have determined whether or not a will exists and a personal represenative has been appointed, it is time to start gathering the documents that will be needed to settle the estate, transfer assets, and close accounts. If the deceased person was your spouse, you may have a good idea of where to locate the various documents on this list. It may be a bit more challenging to locate these documents if the decedent was not your spouse or did not reside in your home. Regardless, it is important to start the process of gathering the needed documents.

Get Organized

First, you will want to get organized. You will likely end up with a number of important documents. Obtaining a three-ring binder, or an "accordion" style pocketed folder to keep the various documents organized is a great start. After gathering the initial documents, you will begin accumulating other documents from banks, insurance companies, employers and other organizations. Either the binder or folder will come in handy as a centralized storage spot.

Securing Documents

It is important that you store the folder or binder in a safe place, as it will end up containing a large amount of personal information about the deceased individual. You don't want that information to fall into the wrong hands. You might consider obtaining a lockable fireproof box to store the folder in when you are not actively working on completion of one of the tasks.

Document List

There are a number of documents that will be important for you to gather in the coming days. These documents will be needed as you close accounts, apply for benefits, and make other financial changes. At the right is a list of the documents you might need. Some may or may not apply to your situation. On the succeeding pages you will find a more detailed description of each document and why it might be needed.

Document List

Personal Documents
- ❒ Death Certificate
- ❒ Social Security Number
- ❒ Employer contact information
- ❒ Marriage, birth, and death certificates / adoption papers
- ❒ Military records and discharge papers

Asset Documents
- ❒ Investment or brokerage statements
- ❒ Life Insurance policies
- ❒ Pension, IRA, or retirement statements
- ❒ Certificates of deposit
- ❒ Bank statements, checkbooks & registers
- ❒ Notes receivable
- ❒ Motor vehicle titles

Legal & Tax Documents
- ❒ Will
- ❒ Trust
- ❒ Divorce papers
- ❒ Bankruptcy filings
- ❒ Nuptial agreements
- ❒ Partnership or corporate agreements
- ❒ Deeds and deeds of trust
- ❒ Previous years personal tax returns

Miscellaneous Documents
- ❒ Health insurance papers

Debts and Liability Documentation
- ❒ Safe deposit rental agreement & keys
- ❒ Leases
- ❒ Unpaid bills
- ❒ Notes payable
- ❒ Auto Loans
- ❒ Credit Cards and other unsecured debt
- ❒ Mortgages

Personal Documents

Death Certificate

As discussed in Chapter 1, you will need copies of the death certificate for a variety of purposes. Obtain 10 to 15 original copies, as you may need to provide originals to different organizations. Financial institutions, insurance companies, and other organizations will likely require that you furnish a copy of the death certificate in order to disburse funds or close accounts.

Social Security Number

Social Security Numbers are used by financial institutions and other organizations for tracking purposes. The deceased person's accounts may be tied to her Social Security Number. You will need to notify the Social Security Administration about the person's death in order to discontinue benefits or to claim survivor benefits. This process is discussed in more detail in Chapter 5.

Employer Contact Information

You will want to notify the deceased person's employer of her death. Depending on the nature of the person's employment, you or the decedent's estate may be entitled to income that has not yet been paid, deferred compensation, a retirement pension, or life insurance the employer may have carried on behalf of the individual.

Marriage Certificate, Birth Certificates / Adoption Papers

You may be required to provide proof of marriage to obtain some benefits. If you have underage children that are eligible for benefits from local, state, or federal programs, you may need to prove that the child was the natural born or adopted descendent of the deceased.

Military Records and Discharge Papers

You may have already found military records and discharge papers if you requested Veteran's honors at the funeral. You may also be eligible for a Survivors Pension benefit. This is a tax free financial benefit for low income, un-remarried surviving spouse or unmarried children of a deceased veteran with wartime service.

Asset Documents

List of Assets

Creating a list of the decedent's assets will be important as you settle the estate. If the decedent was your spouse, and you need the assets for income or to draw from in the future, this step is critically important. The list of assets should include everything the deceased owned of value such as: A home, other real estate, automobiles, cash, and investments. The Appendix of this book contains a sample worksheet for creating an asset list.

Life Insurance Policy Information

The decedent may have had a life insurance policy or policies. If so, you will need to have a copy of the policy declaration page, or the name of the insurance company and a contact number. If the decedent was employed, he or she may have had a life insurance policy as an employee benefit. This process is discussed further in Chapter 8.

Pension, IRA, or Retirement Account Statements
The decedent may have had a pension, individual retirement account, or deferred compensation plan. You will need to locate any documentation related to pensions or accounts in order for the estate, a spouse, or other qualified heir to continue to receive benefits.

Investment or Brokerage Account Information
You will want to gather information on brokerage accounts, IRA's, 401k, and any other investment accounts. Like the bank accounts, you will need this in order to access, close, or transfer the account(s). See Chapter 9 for more information.

Certificates of Deposit
Certificates of deposit are time-based deposits offered by banks, credit unions, and other financial institutions. A CD guarantees a specific amount of interest in exchange for keeping the money on deposit with the institution. If you or the owner of a CD withdraws money before the contract is up, a penalty may have to be paid. Some CD's, however, have a provision that allows the estate of a deceased person to withdraw the money without penalty. See Chapter 9 for more information.

Bank Account Information
Prior to contacting the bank, you will need to make a list of the decedent's bank account numbers. If you don't know the account number(s), then the bank may allow you to use the person's Social Security number instead. If possible, it might be helpful to find the decedent's checking account(s) register. This may help you determine some of the decedent's monthly obligations and liabilities.

Notes Receivable
If the decedent made personal loans to friends, family, or business associates, he may have a note receivable with that individual or entity. This money will now be owed to the estate or a named beneficiary. The note receivable will be considered an asset of the estate.

Motor Vehicle Titles
If the deceased owned a motor vehicle, you will want to locate the title or registration. If she owned the vehicle jointly, it will become the property of the other party. If it was owned individually, it will become an asset of the estate.

Legal and Tax Documents

Will
As mentioned in Chapter 2, a will is a person's legal instruction for how to distribute his assets and belongings upon death. These assets and belongings are called an "Estate." If the decedent created a will, you will need this to settle the estate. Additionally, the will may name a Personal Representative or Executor. This is the person that is responsible for handling the Estate.

Trust Documents
In addition to a will, some people create trusts as a way to hold or pass assets to other people, charities, or other entities upon their death. A trust may also "entrust" a certain person or entity to manage assets for the benefit of someone else. This person is called a Trustee. If the decedent's assets were placed in a Trust, it will be important to have a copy of the Trust, in order for the estate to be settled.

Divorce Papers
If the deceased was divorced, there may be stipulations in the divorce settlement that require the estate to give assets to the former spouse. Also, a former spouse may be entitled to receive a portion of a pension or IRA. Locating the divorce settlement agreement will help answer these questions.

Bankruptcy Filings
If the decedent filed for bankruptcy during his lifetime, you will need to locate the bankruptcy documents. This is so that you can determine if there are any unpaid liabilities that were not included in the bankruptcy. You will also be able to prove that accounts have been settled with creditors if by chance a former creditor tries to go after the estate for payment.

Pre-Nuptial Agreements
Some people enter into pre-nuptial agreements prior to getting married. This often occurs when one or both spouses have accumulated significant assets prior to getting married.

Partnership or Corporate Agreements
If the decedent was a partner, member, or shareholder in a business, you will want to locate any documents related to the business. You will need to consult with a business and estate attorney to determine how the business ownership transfers to the estate or other beneficiary.

Deeds and Deeds of Trust
A deed is a written legal instrument that passes ownership of property from one party to another. Typically, deeds are associated with real estate. If the decedent owned a property outright (no mortgage), then she should have a deed associated with that property. The deed will be needed when settling the estate.

Previous Years Personal Tax Returns
You will want to have a copy of the deceased person's pervious years tax returns. This will help you identify assets owned by the decedent. Also, you, or the estate, will be required to file a final tax return. Having a copy of the previous year's return will be helpful in identifying items such as loss carry forwards.

Liabilities/Debt

Having a sense of the decedent's liabilities and debts is important. When you settle the estate, you need to make sure all the creditors are accounted for, and that appropriate action is taken with each. If the deceased person was your spouse, and you are unfamiliar with the household monthly obligations, you also need to know this information.

Chapter 7 discusses obtaining a credit report for the decedent as a part of identity theft protection. A credit report is also a good source of information about debts and liabilities. It will list most debts such as car loans, mortgages, and credit cards. You will, however, also need to consider other liabilities or payments that may not show up on the credit report, such as:

HOA Dues	Membership Dues
Utility Bills	Magazine subscriptions
Auto Insurance	Notes Payable
Cell Phone Contract	

Chapter 10 deals with how to handle debts, liabilities, and other payments. Please refer to the sample Asset & Liability list in the Appendix.

Chapter Summary

***Get Organized*:** Using a binder or folder is a way to keep all of the documents you collect related to the estate organized.

***Secure Documents*:** Make sure you find a secure location to store the documents.

***First Step Resources*:** Use the asset and liability checklists in the appendix of this book to help you keep track of the accounts, investments, debts, and bills.

☑ ***Action Steps***

- ☐ ____________________
- ☐ ____________________
- ☐ ____________________
- ☐ ____________________
- ☐ ____________________
- ☐ ____________________
- ☐ ____________________
- ☐ ____________________
- ☐ ____________________
- ☐ ____________________
- ☐ ____________________
- ☐ ____________________
- ☐ ____________________
- ☐ ____________________
- ☐ ____________________
- ☐ ____________________
- ☐ ____________________
- ☐ ____________________
- ☐ ____________________

____

My Notes

Chapter 4: Hiring Professional Advisors

You may have a great set of financial and legal advisors in place to assist you with the various tasks associated with handling the deceased person's affairs. Many people, however, don't have a dependable team in place. If you are in this situation, then this will be an important chapter for you to read and understand.

Depending on your situation, you may need to hire professional advisors such as a financial advisor, estate/probate attorney, or tax accountant. This chapter will help you understand what each of these professionals does, how they might be of assistance to you, and what questions to ask when deciding to hire a professional. This chapter looks at the three primary types of advisors you may need to engage for help: Financial Advisor, Estate/ Probate Attorney, and CPA/Accountant.

Financial Advisors

What does a Financial Advisor do?

At the very basic level, a financial advisor helps clients pick different investment vehicles in which money is invested. An advisor may help an individual pick stocks, bonds, or mutual funds. Some advisors also manage a portfolio of individual stocks. An advisor may also work with a client to create a budget and a long-term financial plan. Others may do all of this as well as assist with life insurance and estate planning.

Why might I need a Financial Advisor?

If you are an experienced investor, you may not need the assistance of a Financial Advisor. If finances are not your strong suit, then you may consider seeking the help of a Financial Advisor. Additionally, if the decedent's death resulted in a significant inheritance or life insurance payout, it would be wise to retain the assistance of an advisor to determine the best way to invest the proceeds.

Are there different types of Financial Advisors?

There are a variety of different types of financial advisors including: stock brokers, registered representatives, and Certified Financial Planners. Advisors may be affiliated with a broker/dealer, part of a bank, or with an independent firm. Advisors are compensated differently depending on the type of firm they work for and the platform they operate on.

How are Financial Advisors compensated?

- **Brokers** that work for a broker/dealer are typically compensated with a commission when their client buys or sells a specific investment.

- **Registered Representatives** typically work on a fee-only basis, which means that they are paid a flat-fee or fee based on the percentage of assets a client has with the advisor.

- **Certified Financial Planners** may charge a flat-fee to create a financial plan for a client. A CFP may then receive either commissions as a broker or work on a fee-only basis as a registered representative to implement the investment plan.

What questions should I ask when hiring a Financial Advisor?

To the right, you will find a list of questions to ask when interviewing financial advisors. This text was taken directly from the Securities and Exchange Commission website

Most investment advisers must fill out a form called "Form ADV." They must file their Form ADV's with either the SEC or the state securities agency in the state where they have their principal place of business, depending on the amount of assets they manage.

Form ADV consists of two parts. Part 1 contains information about the adviser's business and whether they've had problems with regulators or clients. Part 2 outlines the adviser's services, fees, and strategies. Before you hire someone to be your investment adviser, always ask for, and carefully read, both parts of Form ADV.

You can get copies of Form ADV by accessing the Investment Adviser Public Disclosure (IAPD) website at http://www.adviserinfo.sec.gov/.

You can also get copies of Form ADV from the investment adviser, your state securities regulator or the SEC, depending on the size of the adviser's portfolio. You can find out how to get in touch with your state securities regulator through the North American Securities Administrators Association, Inc.'s (NASAA) website or by calling (202) 737-0900. Ask your state securities regulator whether they've had any complaints about the adviser.

Important questions to ask when choosing financial advisors

- ❐ What experience do you have, especially with people in my circumstances?
- ❐ Where did you go to school? What is your recent employment history?
- ❐ What licenses do you hold? Are you registered with the SEC, a state, or the Financial Industry Regulatory Authority (FINRA)?
- ❐ What products and services do you offer?
- ❐ Can you only recommend a limited number of products or services to me? If so, why?
- ❐ How are you paid for your services? What is your usual hourly rate, flat fee, or commission?
- ❐ Have you ever been disciplined by any government regulator for unethical or improper conduct or been sued by a client who was not happy with the work you did?
- ❐ For registered investment advisers, will you send me a copy of both parts of your Form ADV?
- ❐ Be sure to meet potential advisers "face to face" to make sure you get along. And remember: there are many types of individuals who can help you develop a personal financial plan and manage your hard–earned money.

Source Securities and Exchange Commissionwww.sec.gov

Accountant or Tax Professional

What does an accountant or tax professional do?

An accountant or tax professional can assist you in preparing tax returns. They can also assist with tax planning, estate planning, and more.

Why might I need an accountant or tax professional?

If the decedent owned a business or a real estate portfolio, or if the estate involves a significant amount of gifting and inheritance, retaining a professional accountant will likely be necessary.

Are there different types of accountants and tax professionals?

Yes. There are bookkeepers, tax preparers, accountants, and Certified Public Accountants (CPA). A bookkeeper or tax preparer can likely assist you with filing a very basic tax return for the decedent. If the situation is more complex, you will want the assistance of an accountant. An accountant with the CPA designation adheres to stringent qualification standards and licensing requirements.

How are accountants and tax professionals compensated?

Tax professionals may bill by the hour, form, overall return or some combination. After reviewing your previous returns and interviewing you, a tax professional should be able to give you a good-faith estimate of costs. If the CPA uses a time-based system, discuss the hourly rate of the accountant and staff, overhead expense reimbursement, and whether certain time is not billed. Find out now whether a simple two-minute phone call or a one-page fax means an hour of billable time.

Important questions to ask when choosing a Certified Public Accountant

- ❒ Does the individual hold an active CPA license?
- ❒ Are your needs compatible with the CPA's personality and communication style?
- ❒ Does the CPA have the experience you need?
- ❒ It's important to establish a practitioner's credentials before you retain his or her services. You need to feel that this person has integrity and honesty before you will trust him or her with your financial information. Be aware that fee structures vary and that different types of practitioners have different levels of training and experience.
- ❒ Ask your lawyer, banker, insurance agent, or investment advisor for recommendations.
- ❒ Make sure the CPA is licensed to practice in your state.
- ❒ Ask what professional organizations the CPA belongs to and how active he or she is in those organizations. Many of these organizations require adherence to technical and professional standards, thereby helping to ensure the quality of a CPA's services.

Probate Attorney

What does an Probate attorney do?

Probate attorneys specialize in estate mediation. They open probate cases, submit decedent wills through the court system, and provide assistance to the designated probate executor or personal representative.

Why might I need an Probate attorney?

Probate is required within each of the 50 states unless individuals establish a revocable or irrevocable trust. The probate process is required to validate a decedent's last will and testament, estate settlement, and distribution of inheritance assets to designated heirs. When family discord exists, a probate litigator may be required. Transactional probate lawyers are usually required when decedents die without leaving a will.

Are there different types Probate attorneys?

Any attorney that has passed the bar and is appropriately licensed in your state may act as a probate attorney. Like physicians, however, most attorneys tend to develop a specialty in a certain area of the law.

Important questions to ask when choosing a Probate Attorney

- ❒ Does your practice focus on trusts and estates, including estate planning, estate administration, and estate litigation?
- ❒ How many years of experience do you have?
- ❒ Are you properly licensed in my state?
- ❒ Do you possess a broad range of experience and knowledge relating to trusts and estates?
- ❒ Do you charge a flat fee or an hourly rate for providing estate and probate services?
- ❒ What are the potential problems with my case?
- ❒ Ask yourself: "Can I see myself working closely with this attorney?"

How are estate/probate attorneys compensated?

Probate attorneys are typically compensated in one of three different ways: By the hour, a flat-fee, or based on a percentage of the value of the estate's assets.

Hourly –Hourly fees vary depending your geographic location and the attorney's training and experience. An attorney that specializes in estate planning and probate will likely charge a little more per hour than a generalist, but you will get a specialist that should know probate law inside out.

Flat-Fee – This method has become a common practice for many probate attorneys. By charging a flat fee, the attorney does not have to track every minute spent on a case and the client has a better sense of how much probate will cost. A flat-fee arrangement may exclude court filing costs, recording costs, and appraisals.

Percentage of Estate Value – In this arrangement, you pay the probate attorney a percentage of the total assets in the estate. This is the least desirable fee arrangement because it is the most costly.

Chapter Summary

Determine Your Need: Determine why you need a professional advisor.

Understand Which Questions to Ask: You may be able to save yourself time, money, and frustration by knowing which questions to ask a prospective advisor.

Seek Referrals: Seek referrals from friends and family of advisors that they trust with their personal finances and legal issues.

☑ ***Action Steps***

- ☐ ______________________________
- ☐ ______________________________
- ☐ ______________________________
- ☐ ______________________________
- ☐ ______________________________
- ☐ ______________________________
- ☐ ______________________________
- ☐ ______________________________
- ☐ ______________________________
- ☐ ______________________________
- ☐ ______________________________
- ☐ ______________________________
- ☐ ______________________________
- ☐ ______________________________
- ☐ ______________________________
- ☐ ______________________________
- ☐ ______________________________
- ☐ ______________________________
- ☐ ______________________________

My Notes

Part II: Notifications

Part II addresses the notifications that need to be taken, regardless of who has passed away. This section is divided into seven chapters. Each chapter addresses a unique concept.

Chapter 5: Social Security Notification and Benefits

This chapter will help you understand the basics of filing for social security survivor benefits for yourself or other dependents.

Chapter 6: Notifying Employers and Other Organizations

Employers and other organizations need to be notified of the decedent's death. This chapter outlines various issues that need to be addressed with this type of notification.

Chapter 7: Identity Protection

Identity theft among the deceased is one of the fastest growing forms of fraud in the United States. This chapter will help you understand how to better prevent a deceased person's identity from being stolen.

Chapter 8: Life Insurance Claims

Life insurance and filing for claims can be a very confusing process. This chapter provides an overview of different types of life insurance and how to start the claims process.

Chapter 9: Bank and Investment Accounts

This chapter outlines the various ways bank and investment accounts can be held, and how you should go about closing or transferring an account.

Chapter 10: Liabilities and Debt

People often die with liabilities and other debt. This chapter will help you understand what types of debt an estate might be liable for and those for which the estate may have no liability.

Chapter 11: Email, Social Media, and Internet Accounts

The rise of the email, social media, and the internet have created a new class of "digital assets." This chapter will help you understand the rules for accessing these assets.

Chapter 5: Social Security Notification and Benefits Eligibility

When a person dies, the Social Security Administration needs to be notified of the death. Often, the funeral home that has cared for the deceased person will make the appropriate notification to the Social Security Administration. It is important to ask the funeral director if this has been done on your behalf. While the funeral home may have made the official notification, you will still need to file directly for survivor benefits.

Social Security Survivor Benefits

The Social Security Administration provides two types of benefits when a worker dies: One-Time Death Benefit and Monthly Survivor Benefits

- *One-Time Death Benefit*: Assuming the deceased person had enough work credits at the time of death, the surviving spouse or dependent children can claim the One Time Death Benefit. The benefit amount is small, only $255 as of October 2012. If you are entitled to it, however, you should make a claim.

- *Monthly Survivor Benefits:* Dependent children, surviving spouses, and even ex-spouses may be entitled to monthly survivor benefits. The deceased person does not have to have been of retirement age in order for benefits to be paid.

How Social Security Benefits Work

Social Security Benefits are based on the number of credits a worker has earned. Generally speaking, a worker can earn up to four credits per year. A worker needs 40 credits, or about 10 years worth of work, in order to qualify for Social Security Benefits. There are exceptions to this rule: If the deceased person had not accumulated 40 credits, benefits may still be paid to the surviving spouse and dependent children. If the deceased person had accumulated at least six credits (one and a half years work), over the previous three years, then benefits may be paid. Also, if the deceased person was already receiving retirement or disability benefits, the Social Security Administration will pay the survivors based on those benefits. In other words, no new credits are needed to qualify.

Benefits for Widows, Widowers, and Former Spouses
If you are the widow or widower of a person who worked long enough to receive Social Security there are several options:

- You may receive the decedent's full benefits when you reach full retirement age.

- You may begin receiving benefits at age 50 if you are disabled and the disability started before the worker's death.

- You may receive benefits at any age if you are caring for the deceased worker's child who is under the age of 16.

If you are a former spouse, you may qualify for benefits just the same as a widow or widower. The marriage had to last for at least 10 years or more.

Benefits for Minor or Disabled Children

- If a child is unmarried and under the age of 18, that child may be eligible to receive Social Security survivor benefits.

- If the child is disabled prior to the age of 22, he or she may also qualify for benefits.

- In some cases a deceased worker's stepchildren, grandchildren, or adopted children may receive benefits.

Calculating Survivor Benefits

The survivor benefit amount is based on the earnings of the deceased person. The more the person paid into Social Security while alive, the higher the benefits will be. The monthly benefits are a percentage of the deceased worker's basic Social Security benefit.

Beyond the information mentioned above, there are a variety of factors that go into determining the monthly benefit amount. For more detailed information on how the amount is calculated, please visit http://www.socialsecurity.gov/survivorplan

Termination of Benefits

If the deceased person was already receiving Social Security benefits, and she does not have a widow, widower, or dependent child, you will need to notify the Social Security Administration of her death. Once a person has passed away, it is unlawful to continue to receive benefits, unless there is a rightful beneficiary. If you don't report the death to the Social Security Administration promptly, they may demand benefit payments back retroactively. According to the Social Security Administration website, "Eligibility for benefits ends with the month in which the recipient dies. Payments are terminated effective with the month after the month of death".

Starting the process to claim Social Security Benefits

To get the process started for receipt of benefits, you may go to the Social Security Administration website at www.ssa.gov or call 800-772-1213. While you can start a portion of the benefits claim process online or over the phone, you will ultimately need to visit your local social security office before benefits are paid.

Chapter Summary

Notification: Often, funeral homes will assist you with notifying the Social Security Administration of a death. Ask the funeral director that cared for the decedent if this was done on your behalf.

Benefits: You or a dependent of the deceased may be eligible for a one-time survivor benefit or monthly survivor benefits. You will need to contact the Social Security Administration to see if you or a dependent qualifies. You must file in person.

☑ ***Action Steps***

- ☐ ______________________________
- ☐ ______________________________
- ☐ ______________________________
- ☐ ______________________________
- ☐ ______________________________
- ☐ ______________________________
- ☐ ______________________________
- ☐ ______________________________
- ☐ ______________________________
- ☐ ______________________________
- ☐ ______________________________
- ☐ ______________________________
- ☐ ______________________________
- ☐ ______________________________
- ☐ ______________________________
- ☐ ______________________________
- ☐ ______________________________
- ☐ ______________________________
- ☐ ______________________________
- ☐ ______________________________

My Notes

Chapter 6: Notifying Employers and Other Organizations

Notifying Current Employer

If the deceased person was employed, you will need to notify his employer of the death. Depending on the size of the employer, you may have to work through the human resource administrator. If the employer was smaller in size, you may work directly with the owner of the business. Regardless of the type of company, you will want to do the following:

Final Pay & Other Compensation

Inquire about a final paycheck. As a part of the final paycheck, ask about:

- Back pay
- Accrued paid time off
- Sick pay
- Bonuses or commissions that are due

Cancel Direct Deposit

If the paycheck was deposited via direct deposit, you will need to make sure that you ask the human resource contact to cancel the direct deposit (or ACH transfer), once the final check is paid. This is important because direct deposits or ACH transfers can also be used to withdraw money from an account.

Business Expenses

If the deceased person had an expense account and used a personal credit card for monthly business expenses, you will need to work with the human resource contact to complete a final expense report, so that you or the estate can be reimbursed for any out of pocket business expenses that were incurred prior to death.

Continuation of Health Benefits (COBRA)

Depending on how the employer health benefits are structured, it may be possible to continue coverage of dependent health benefits for a specific period of time. In 1986, Congress mandated under the Consolidated Omnibus Budget Reconciliation Act (COBRA) that group health benefits are required to be continued for employees or their dependents after specific events. Among the events that qualify for continuation is the death of an employee.

If the employer has 20 or more employees in a group health plan, the employer is required to offer COBRA. COBRA is generally more expensive than coverage for active employees. With COBRA you will be responsible for covering the entire health premium. The state or local government usually sponsors COBRA. For more information about COBRA consult your state's Department of Insurance. In the appendix of this book you will find web links and phone numbers for each state's Department of Insurance

If the employer has fewer than 20 people, there may not be an option for continued health insurance coverage. Talk the to company's human resource contact to determine what options are available.

Group Life Insurance Benefits

Many employers offer group life insurance benefits at no cost to the employee. Group term life insurance provides protection for a specific period of time and pays a benefit only if the insured dies during the term. There is no cash value buildup in a term life insurance policy. The death benefit is paid income tax free to the beneficiary.

401k, 403b, 457b, and Deferred Compensation Plans

Chapter 9 addresses what to do with qualified retirement plans such as 401k's. At this point, it is just important that you find out if the person had an employer sponsored retirement account and how you should go about contacting the administrator of the account. 401k plans are offered by private sector employers; 403b plans are offered by employers in the nonprofit arena; and, 457b plans are offered by state employers. Also, some private sector employers offer deferred compensation plans. Depending on the structure of the deferred compensation plans, the beneficiary or heir may be entitled to monthly, quarterly, or annual income payments. There may also be a feature that allows for a one-time lump sum cash distribution.

Personal Belongings

You will want to set up a time to retrieve the decedent's belongings from the workplace. If it is too difficult for you to visit the employer, ask that the personal belongings be delivered to you directly.

Notifying Pervious Employers & Other Organizations

You may also want to contact previous employers via phone or letter to inquire about any old retirement accounts, stock, or other assets that may not have been moved after the employee left that company.

Below is a list of other organizations that you may want to notify when you have the time and energy. The organization may want to announce the decedents death. Or you may want to have the person removed from mailing lists.

- College Alumni Associations
- Fraternal Organizations
- Professional Associations & Unions
- Religious Groups
- Political Groups

Chapter Summary

Notify Current Employer: Contact the decedent's current employer to make arrangements for final pay, reimbursable business expenses, and the receipt of personal belongings.

Continuation of Benefits: If the decedent had dependents, talk with the company or the Department of Insurance about continuation of medical benefits.

Other Notifications: You may want to notify previous employers and other organizations so the decedent can be listed in memoriam or be removed from mailing lists.

☑ *Action steps*

- ☐ ____________________
- ☐ ____________________
- ☐ ____________________
- ☐ ____________________
- ☐ ____________________
- ☐ ____________________
- ☐ ____________________
- ☐ ____________________
- ☐ ____________________
- ☐ ____________________
- ☐ ____________________
- ☐ ____________________
- ☐ ____________________
- ☐ ____________________
- ☐ ____________________
- ☐ ____________________
- ☐ ____________________
- ☐ ____________________
- ☐ ____________________
- ☐ ____________________

My Notes

Chapter 7: Identity Protection

There is a new type of financial fraud that is growing at an exponential rate in the United States. This fraud is the theft of an identity from deceased a person. According to a report released by San Diego based ID Analytics in April, 2012, nearly 2.5 million deceased people in the United States have their identities misused each year. The study indicates:

> *"800,000 deceased American's identities are intentionally targeted for misuse on applications for credit products and cell phone service. In approximately 1.6 million applications annually, an identity manipulator used the SSN of a deceased person."*

Fraud artists use stolen identities to apply for credit, open credit cards, obtain auto loans, and various other crimes. These identity theft crimes not only mar the name of the deceased person, they can also create problems for the deceased victim's estates and for surviving family members.

Ways to Minimize Identity Theft for the Deceased Persons

There are six steps you need to take to help prevent identity theft of the deceased. Each of these steps is discussed in detail below:

Six Ways to Minimize The Theft of a Deceased Persons Identity

1. Limit Obituary Information
2. Gather and Secure Financial Documents
3. Notify Credit Reporting Agencies
4. Notify the Social Security Administration
5. Cancel Driver's License
6. Notify Financial Entities

Step 1: Limit Obituary Information
As mentioned in Chapter 1, publicly available obituaries can be a source of information for criminals who are intent on stealing the identity of a recently deceased person. Limiting the amount of personal information in an obituary will reduce the chance of a deceased person's identity being stolen. Please see Chapter 1 for more detailed information.

Step 2: Gather and Secure Financial Documents
As mentioned in Chapter 2, you will want to gather documents for the purpose of assessing assets, liabilities, income, and account closure. It is also important to gather financial documents for protection purposes. By gathering and securing documents in a central location, you can prevent people with ill intent from having access to sensitive information. Sadly, in many cases, a family member steals the identity of the deceased person. For this reason, it is best to gather and secure the decedent's information, and limit the number of people who have access to that information.

Step 3: Notify Credit Reporting Agencies

The proliferation of identity theft for both the living and the deceased has resulted in the creation of procedures by the three major credit-reporting agencies to help prevent the unauthorized use of credit.

- Immediately notify the three primary credit-reporting agencies (Experian, Equifax, and TransUnion,) of the person's death. You will want to call the agencies and then follow up with a letter. Contact information for each agency has been provided in the Appendix at the end of this book.

- Request that his file be marked with a *Deceased Do Not Issue Credit*

- Request a copy of the decedent's credit report. This will help you in determining which other financial institutions you need to contact.

- Make all requests in writing and send via certified mail. This will provide you with a paper trail in case an account is opened after you notify the agencies. You will want to include an official or certified copy of the death certificate in your correspondence with the Credit Reporting Agencies.

Step 4: Notify the Social Security Administration

In Chapter 5, the need to notify the Social Security Administration was discussed. This is important because the social Security Administration will flag the decedents Social Security Number as deceased. This will make it more difficult for an identity thief to utilize the number.

Step 5: Cancel Driver's License or Identification Card

Driver's Licenses and state issued ID cards are the primary source of identification for individuals in the United States. Many states allow for renewal of licenses and ID cards by mail. It is important to have the decedent removed from the state's DMV mailing list and to cancel his card. Some states will allow you to mail a certified copy of the death certificate, along with a letter or explanation. Others require that you go to the DMV in person and make the request.

In addition to canceling the driver's license or ID card, you will also want to cancel any disabled placards or license plates, and transfer ownership and registration of vehicles that were in the name of the deceased.

The requirement for cancelation of a license and transferring ownership of vehicles varies by state. In the Reference section at the end of this book, a list of state specific phone numbers and web links, for each DMV has been provided. You can call the DMV or visit its web site for more state specific information.

Step 6: Notify Financial Institutions

Chapters 9 and 10 discuss how to notify financial institutions about the passing of the decedent. You will need to do this for all bank, investment, insurance, credit card, mortgage and other financial institutions with which the deceased had an account.

☙ *Chapter Summary* ❧

Identity Theft Threat: The theft of deceased person's identities is on the rise. It is important to take steps to protect the decedent's identity so that the estate, beneficiaries, and heirs are protected.

Protection Steps: Follow the six-step approach outlined in the chapter to protect the decedent's identity.

☑ ***Action Steps***

- ☐ ______________________________
- ☐ ______________________________
- ☐ ______________________________
- ☐ ______________________________
- ☐ ______________________________
- ☐ ______________________________
- ☐ ______________________________
- ☐ ______________________________
- ☐ ______________________________
- ☐ ______________________________
- ☐ ______________________________
- ☐ ______________________________
- ☐ ______________________________
- ☐ ______________________________
- ☐ ______________________________
- ☐ ______________________________
- ☐ ______________________________
- ☐ ______________________________
- ☐ ______________________________
- ☐ ______________________________

My Notes

Chapter 8: Life Insurance Claims

A life insurance policy is a contract between two parties: The life insurance company and the policy owner. The life insurance company agrees to pay a death benefit at the time of the insured's death if the policy owner has paid the policy premiums as stipulated in the contract and if the policy is still in force. The policy owner and the insured are often the same person; however, the owner of the policy and the insured do not have to be the same person. The owner could be a spouse, other family member, or even a business entity such as a corporation.

A policy will typically have one or more beneficiaries that receive the proceeds or "death benefit" when the insured person passes away. In certain circumstances, the beneficiary of a policy may be a business that the insured person owned, a charitable organization, or other entity. For the purposes of this book, please assume that you or a family member is the beneficiary(s) of the decedent's policy.

Types of Life Insurance Policies

All life insurance policies fall under one of two broad categories: Term and Permanent Insurance. Term insurance is designed for people who only want life insurance for a specific period of time, while permanent insurance can provide lifelong protection.

- **Term Insurance** is insurance that is set up for a specific amount of time. Usually, term insurance is sold in 10, 15, 20, and 30 year term periods. In order for you to receive the death benefit associated with a term policy, the policy must still be in force. This means that the monthly or annual payments have been made on time according to the contract. Also, the term of the contract cannot have expired.

- **Permanent Life Insurance** has a death benefit like term insurance, but with some key differences. With permanent life insurance, the insured person can borrow against the cash value of the life insurance policy. If the decedent borrowed against the cash value of the policy while he was alive, and the loan has an outstanding balance at death, then that loan balance will be deducted from the proceeds of the death benefit. A Permanent Life policy may be referred to as a Whole Life, Universal Life, or Variable Life Policy.

Information Needed for the Claims Process

In order to make a life insurance claim, you will need to have several pieces of information to start the claims process. Below is a list of what most insurance companies will need in order to begin:

- Insured person's full name
- Date of birth
- State of residence
- Copy of the life insurance policy or the policy number

- Date and cause of death
- Name of person reporting the claim, and her relationship to the deceased
- Your contact information (phone/email)
- Original copy of death certificate

Contacting the Agent or Carrier

Once you have collected the above referenced information, you will need to contact either your insurance agent or the carrier of the policy. If you do not know who the agent or carrier is, there are several search services that can help try to locate the decedent's policy carrier:

- **www.FindYourPolicy.com** is a service that attempts to locate life insurance policies on behalf of beneficiaries. At the time of publication, the service charged $9.95 to search its database. The catch with this service is that the policy would have to have been registered by the insured person.

- **MIB Solutions** offers an insurance policy search service. At the time of publication, MIB charged $75 per search, per search of over 180 million policy records. The company claims a 30% success rate in locating policies. You can access their service by going to http://www.mibsolutions.com/lost-life-insurance/

The Claims Filing Process

Once you contact the agent or insurance carrier, he will request the information listed above. You can usually get the process started over the phone or online with some carriers. The insurance company will send you a package of claim forms that you will need to complete and return along with an original copy of the death certificate. **Make sure to send this package of information back by certified mail**. This will create a paper trail and provide proof that you sent the information, should a problem arise down the road.

If there are multiple adult beneficiaries, each adult will need to file his own claim. Additionally, if the primary beneficiary died before the death of the policyholder, then the contingent (or alternate) beneficiary can make a claim for the proceeds of the policy. The contingent beneficiary, however, will need to prove that the primary beneficiary is deceased by providing the death certificate of the primary beneficiary. It may sound complicated but, hopefully, you will not run into this situation.

The claim process can be as short as a week or it can extend as long as several months. It all depends on the nature of the deceased person's death and the insurance company with which you are working.

Contestability

There is a feature of virtually every life insurance policy of which very few people are aware. It is called contestability. Contestability is the process by which an insurance company contests the payment of the death benefit.

Typically, there is a two-year contestability window for insurance companies. At their discretion, the insurance company may initiate an independent investigation into the nature of a person's death. This is done when the insurance company suspects foul play, suicide, or deception at application.

- **Foul Play**: In the case of foul play, the insurance company will want to confirm that a beneficiary of the policy is not involved.

- **Suicide**: Many policies state that the policy is void if a suicide occurs inside of the two-year contestability period.

- **Deception at Application**: If an insured person knowingly lied about his health at the time of application, this could invalidate the insurance policy.

- Statistically, life insurance companies only deny about 1% of death benefits claims.

Payment Method

Once your claim is approved, you will need to decide how you would like to receive your benefits. There are typically two options: A one-time lump sum payment or annual payments over a set period of time.

- **Lump Sum Payments**: Selecting this payment method will give you all of the death benefit proceeds at one time. If you do not feel well qualified to manage this money, plan on engaging a financial advisor. This may also be the best choice should you need to pay off estate debts.

- **Annual Payments**: This payment method is often used for minors or other individuals who are unable to proficiently manage a large amount of money. Typically, the insurance company will reinvest this money and pay the beneficiary the interest on the proceeds.

Other Places to Check

The discussion above has focused on traditional life insurance. There are, however, other potential sources of insurance benefit money that may be paid upon a death:

- **Credit Life Insurance**: This is insurance that is offered as an extra benefit with mortgages and credit cards. Credit Life Insurance will pay off the money owed on a mortgage or other consumer credit facility. The policy would have been issued at the time the credit was taken out.

- **Accidental Death:** If the decedent passed away in an auto related accident, you may be eligible for the auto insurance death benefit. Depending on the situation, this may be paid by your auto insurance company, or the company insuring the other car (if there was one), in an accident.

- **Employer Provided Life Insurance**: Many employers provide life insurance as a part of an overall benefit package. When you contact the deceased person's employer (see Chapter 4), ask the human resource contact if the company carried any life insurance on the deceased. A beneficiary, or the estate, may be entitled to the proceeds.

- **Homeowner's Insurance**: Under certain circumstances, a homeowner's insurance policy may be obligated to pay a death benefit if the deceased person died in an accident at home. The Homeowner's policy would need to have a specific "Rider." Check with the agent or carrier that insured the home.

Chapter Summary

Locate Life Insurance Policy: Locate the life insurance policy and determine the type of policy that was purchased.

Contact Agent or Issuing Company: Contact the agent or insurance company that issued the policy to begin the claims process.

Look for other Insurance Policies: You or another beneficiary may qualify for other life insurance proceeds from employer sponsored policies, accidental death policies, or homeowner's insurance.

☑ **Action Steps**

☐ ____________________

☐ ____________________

☐ ____________________

☐ ____________________

☐ ____________________

☐ ____________________

☐ ____________________

☐ ____________________

☐ ____________________

☐ ____________________

☐ ____________________

☐ ____________________

☐ ____________________

☐ ____________________

☐ ____________________

☐ ____________________

☐ ____________________

☐ ____________________

My Notes

Chapter 9: Banking and Investment Accounts

What happens to bank accounts and investment accounts when a person dies? The answer is, it depends. Below is a discussion on how different types of bank and investment accounts are handled. First, we review how traditional bank accounts, such as checking and savings, are affected when a person dies. Then, we will look at how investment accounts such as brokerage, IRA, and qualified retirement accounts are affected.

Seek Professional Tax Advice

It is highly recommended that you seek professional tax advice when inheriting money, either from depository or investment accounts. The laws governing inheritance and taxation are continually changing. Some investment accounts allow you to take distributions tax free, while you may be required to pay taxes on other types of accounts. Depending on your beneficiary status and relationship to the deceased, you may have access to all of the funds immediately without penalty, or you may only be able to take distributions over a period of time. There are specific rules about retaining the tax-free status of some investments such as Roth IRA's. Therefore, it is best practice to consult with an accountant or a tax planning professional who is knowledgeable about the laws applicable to your specific state.

Bank Accounts

Traditional bank accounts include checking and savings accounts. The manner in which these accounts are "held" or owned will dictate how and when survivors may access the accounts. There are three primary ways depository accounts are held:

- Individual Account
- Joint Account
- Trust Accounts

Individually Held Accounts

If a deceased person was the only account owner listed on an account, the account may not be accessed, closed, or liquidated until the estate is settled. Even if the deceased person has joint accounts with a spouse or another person, an individually held account may not be changed until estate settlement. In some circumstances, a judge may allow access to an account for the payment of final expenses such as funeral and burial services. Written permission from the court must be obtained in order to access the funds.

On occasion, surviving family members are tempted to forge checks on accounts where the account holder is deceased. This is highly discouraged. Not only is it illegal, but it could also create a variety of other legal issues.

Joint Accounts

If a checking, savings, or other depository account is held jointly with a person that is still living, that person has the right to use that account, as well as the right to the assets in the account. The surviving account holder may continue to use the account, close the account, or move the assets to another account. But, the surviving account holder should remember that the money in the account may be subject to state or federal estate taxes. So, it is wise to minimize use of the account assets until you have a good understanding of any taxes that may be due.

Trust Accounts

If a depository account is held in a living trust, the successor trustee named in the trust document can present the death certificate and a copy of the trust to the bank to take over the account.

Notifying the Bank

Regardless of how the account is held (individually, jointly, or in a trust), making deposits into the account is generally not an issue, since anyone can make a deposit into an account. Taking money out of an account is a different story. It is important to make sure this is done properly and with the correct notification to the financial institution. You may only withdraw money if the account is held jointly, or if you have obtained a court order allowing you to withdraw money.

Notification should be made promptly, especially if other people, such as professional caregivers, have been previously authorized to use an ATM or debit card on the account. Below are the steps for notifying a bank:

1. **Initial Notification:** Call the bank and inform a manager of the account holder's death.

2. **Bank Information Request:** The bank will provide you with a list of the specific forms and documentation they will need to take appropriate action on the account (each bank has its own policies and procedures).

3. **Documentation:** You will have to prove both the account holder's death via a death certificate and your authority to act on behalf of the estate. As mentioned in the previous section, if the account is individually held, you will need to provide evidence that you now have authority over the account. If the account was held jointly, the other person or persons on the account will take possession of the account. If it is a trust account, you will need the successor trustee documentation to transfer the account to the new trustee.

4. **Disbursement:** Once you have determined the type of account and satisfied the bank's documentation requirements, you will need to direct the bank on how to disburse the funds. In the case of an individually held account, you may want to transfer the funds to an estate account to cover final bills, etc. In the case of a jointly held or a trust account, there is no need to close the account, as the other owner has full access to the funds. If, however, the money is going into another account, or into another account at a different bank, you will need to supply the current bank with the new account information. If you are a beneficiary of the account, the bank can write a check directly to you.

Investment Accounts

Investment Accounts are generally set up differently from bank depository accounts. When an investment account such as a certificate of deposit, brokerage, 401k or IRA are set up, often a beneficiary of the account is named. When a beneficiary is named, the account becomes payable directly to that individual or entity. Therefore, the beneficiary does not have to go through the probate process in order to access the funds.

401k and IRA Accounts

If the deceased person was married, usually the person's spouse was named as the beneficiary at the time the account was set up. In fact, the spouse would have to have agreed in writing, at the time the 401k was set up, if a different beneficiary were to be named. If the individual was single, she may have named a family member, friend or charitable entity as the beneficiary of the account. You will need to contact the administrator or investment advisor that holds the accounts. That entity will be able to tell you who the beneficiary is and how you go about transferring the funds. You will likely need to provide evidence of death as well as documentation proving that you are the rightful beneficiary.

Non-Retirement Investment Accounts

State law, not federal law, dictates how securities such as stocks, bonds, and mutual funds are registered and transferred. Nearly every state, however, has adopted the Uniform Transfer-on-Death Securities Registration Act. This Act allows a person to pass securities directly to another person or entity upon death, without having to go through the probate process if a TOD designee was named. Typically, you will need to provide a copy of the death certificate and complete an application of re-registration with the transfer agent. As of the printing of this book, every state except Texas has adopted this Act.

Chapter Summary

Seek Professional Advice: Before distributing any money from bank or investment accounts seek professional advice on how receipt of the assets will affect your taxes.

Bank Accounts: Make a list of all bank accounts. Determine ownership.

Notification: Notify the bank of the decedent's death and make arrangements to close or transfer the accounts.

Investment Accounts: Contact the investment advisor or account custodian. Notify him of the death and make arrangements for the beneficiary to receive proceeds from the account.

☑ ***Actions Steps***

- ☐ ______________________________
- ☐ ______________________________
- ☐ ______________________________
- ☐ ______________________________
- ☐ ______________________________
- ☐ ______________________________
- ☐ ______________________________
- ☐ ______________________________
- ☐ ______________________________
- ☐ ______________________________
- ☐ ______________________________
- ☐ ______________________________
- ☐ ______________________________
- ☐ ______________________________
- ☐ ______________________________
- ☐ ______________________________
- ☐ ______________________________
- ☐ ______________________________
- ☐ ______________________________

My Notes

Chapter 10: Liabilities and Debt

One of the fears that many people have after the death of a family member is that the deceased person's debts will become the liability of the survivors. This is not always the case. In this chapter, we will review how various types of debts and liabilities are treated, and how you should handle them.

As mentioned in Chapter 1, it is a good idea to first get a copy of the deceased person's credit report. Most large banks and consumer finance companies report debts to the three major credit bureaus. The credit report will indicate if the debt is held individually or jointly. These forms of debt holding are treated very differently for deceased persons. It is important to understand the differences, so that you know what your actual liability may be.

Individual Debt

Individual debt is debt that is held in only one person's name. This is sometimes the case with a married couple, where the primary (or only) wage earner qualified for the mortgage with her income and debt only. It is possible for more than one person to have title to an asset, such as a house, but with only one of the persons being held liable for the debt.

Does this mean you can stop paying your mortgage if your deceased spouse or partner was the only person on the loan? Yes. But, it also means the bank that financed the mortgage has the right to foreclose on the house. There would be no financial repercussions to you for stopping payment on the home, but you would also lose the right to live in that home.

Joint Debt

Joint debt is debt that is held in more than one person's name. In the example above, two people held title to the home, but only one person had the liability for the debt. With joint debt, both parties have liability for the loan. So, if you stopped paying on a mortgage that you held jointly with your deceased spouse or partner, in addition to losing the home, you would have financial repercussions that would affect your credit.

Debts such as auto loans, credit cards and other consumer debt that are held solely in the name of the deceased, are not the responsibility of the surviving family members. Creditors may become aggressive when trying to get paid. It is wise not to make any commitments to assume any debt until you know your legal rights and have a clear understanding of what your actual obligation is to the creditor. Creditors know this and will often try to get grieving people to agree to take on debts that they have no obligation to cover. In reality, creditors need to place a claim with the Probate Court to get paid on any individual debts.

If there are not enough assets to cover the liabilities of the estate, creditors are notified that the estate is insolvent. At that point, they write off the liabilities owed. Children, friends, or relatives cannot inherit debt. A credit card company can't legally force someone else to pay the liability of a deceased person.

Changes in How Debt of the Deceased is Handled

There have been two recent changes in federal law that have altered how collections are handled after death:

> **Credit CARD Act of 2009:** The Act requires the executor of an estate to be informed quickly of a collection amount, and requires credit card issuers to stop adding fees and penalties during the time the estate is being settled. That portion of the law went into effect in February 2010.
>
> **FTC Guidelines**: The Federal Trade Commission, in July, 2011, issued a series of guidelines for debt collection from decedents' friends and relatives. The rules represent the FTC's effort to find a middle ground allowing legitimate collection activity while reining in overaggressive collection tactics.

Other Liabilities

In addition to the liabilities you find on the credit report, you will want to look for other monthly payments or bills that may exist. Looking through bank statements, check registers, and credit card statements may reveal monthly re-occurring charges from different entities. Look for payments related to:

- HOA dues
- Utility payments
- Homeowners & Auto insurance
- Cell phone payments
- Membership dues to gyms, clubs, or other organizations
- Newspaper and magazine subscriptions
- Online subscriptions to various web sites or social media outlets.

It may take some time to piece together the various liabilities. But, it is wise to let creditors know as soon as you discover a liability so that you or the estate does not encounter unnecessary interest, fines, or penalties.

Chapter Summary

Make a list of all known debt: Obtain a copy of the decedent's credit report, review check registers and credit card statements for monthly obligations.

Determine how the debt is held: Determine if the debt is individual or joint, as this will be a factor in the requirement for repayment.

Notify creditors: Notify the creditors of the decedent's debt so that additional interest and other fees are not charged.

Don't make any commitments to bill collectors: Before signing anything or committing to repayment of any debt, get all the information. Consult with an attorney for professional legal advice.

☑ ***Actions Steps***

- ☐
- ☐
- ☐
- ☐
- ☐
- ☐
- ☐
- ☐
- ☐
- ☐
- ☐
- ☐
- ☐
- ☐
- ☐
- ☐
- ☐
- ☐
- ☐

My Notes

Chapter 11: Email, Social Media, and Internet Accounts

Prior to the digital era, a person's estate consisted primarily of real personal assets such as investments, real estate and personal property. With the growth of email, social media, and the Internet as important forms of communication, a new asset class has emerged called "digital assets." These digital assets can include important emails, photos, documents and much more.

Determining Site Membership

The first step is to determine which sites or services the decedent used. This can be done by looking through the Internet browser bookmarks or the browser history. Make a list of the sites that the decedent frequented. You may get lucky, as a number of people have automatic logins set up for sites they frequent.

Accessing Sites

Digital assets have really only come into existence in the last twenty years. Because this class of asset is relatively new, there is no standard which every company must follow when it comes to giving survivors access to contents. Each email service or social media outlet has it's own method of handling accounts for deceased persons. Below is a discussion on how some of the more popular email providers and social media sites handle accounts when a person dies. If the decedent used a different service, please check with that service's customer service department for specific instructions.

Gmail

Gmail accounts will stay open forever unless a deceased person's next of kin requests that the account be closed. To get access to the account, you will need to supply the following information by fax or mail to Google:

- Your full name
- Your physical mailing address
- Your email address
- Photocopy of your government issued ID or driver's license
- The Gmail address of the deceased person
- An email containing the full headers of an email message that the deceased person previously emailed to you, with the entire contents of the email.
- The death certificate of the deceased person.

Mail or fax this information to:

Google, Inc.
Gmail User Support – Decedents Accounts
c/o Google Custodian of Records
1600 Amphitheatre Parkway
Mountain View, CA 94043
Fax 650-6440358

After you have sent this information to Google, they will verify the validity and give you access to the account. For additional information or help go to: http://support.google.com

Windows Live/Hotmail/MSN

Microsoft will provide next of kin with a DVD copy of emails in the account of a deceased user. In order to prove that you are legal next of kin, and that the account holder is deceased, Microsoft will require the following documentation:

- An official death certificate for the user
- A document showing that you are the user's next of kin, such as a marriage certificate or power of attorney document
- A copy of a will or trust document naming you as executor or beneficiary
- A birth certificate for the user, if you are his parent; or guardianship paperwork for legal guardians
- A photocopy of your government issued photo ID

You will also need the following information about the account holder:

- Email address or addresses
- First and last name the account holder used when creating the account
- Account holder's date of birth
- City, state, and zip code for the account holder
- Approximately when the account was created
- Approximately when was the account was last accessed
- Your mailing address, if you are requesting a copy of the contents of the account
- What type of computer you use, if you are requesting a copy of the contents of the account (PC, Mac, or Linux)

Once you have collected this information, there are three ways you can send this to Microsoft:

- You may scan and email the documentation to msrecord@microsoft.com.
- You may fax the documentation to (425) 708-7851.
- You may mail copies of the documentation to:

Next of Kin, One Microsoft Way, Redmond, WA 98052

Yahoo

Yahoo will not provide anyone with access to a deceased user's account. They consider this a violation of the user's privacy. They will, however, assist with closing the account.

You must provide a letter containing your request for closure of the account. The letter must include the following:

- The Yahoo user ID
- A copy of a document appointing the requesting party as the personal representative or executor of the deceased person's estate
- A copy of the death certificate of the Yahoo account holder

This information may be mailed or faxed to:

> The Legal Department
> 701 First Avenue
> Sunnyvale, CA 94089-0703
> Fax (408) 349-7941

Facebook

It is Facebook's policy to memorialize the account of a deceased person. For privacy reasons, Facebook will not provide the login information for an account. Once the account has been memorialized, however, Facebook will take measures to secure the account.

To memorialize a Facebook account, go to the help dropdown in Facebook. Type, "deceased," and a link will be brought up that will allow you to request that the profile be memorialized.

You can a request that a Facebook account be removed by searching in the help feature for "request the removal" of a loved one's account. You will be taken to a link for the, "Deceased User's – Special Request" form. This form will request several pieces of information and ask you to upload a scanned copy of the death certificate or power of attorney.

Twitter

In the event of the death of a Twitter user, Twitter will work with a person authorized to act on the behalf of the estate, or with a verified immediate family member of the deceased, to have an account deactivated.

In order for Twitter to process an account deactivation, you must provide the following information:

- The Twitter account's username (e.g., @username or twitter.com/username)
- A copy of the deceased user's death certificate
- A copy of your government-issued ID (e.g., driver's license)
- A signed, notarized statement including:

- Your first and last name
- Your current contact information
- Your email address
- Your relationship to the deceased user
- Action requested (e.g., 'please deactivate the Twitter account')
- A link to an online obituary or a copy of the obituary from a local newspaper (optional)

You may send the documentation by fax or mail to the following address:

> Twitter, Inc.
> c/o: Trust & Safety
> 1355 Market St., Suite 900
> San Francisco, CA 94103
> Fax : 1-415-222-9958

Linked In

Linked In, the business social networking site, has a relatively easy online process for closing a deceased person's profile. Go to http://help.linkedin.com. In the search box, enter "deceased." This will bring up a link to a form that you can complete and submit online.

MySpace

MySpace will not allow access, or update the login information, for a profile for any reason to protect the privacy of the creator of the account. MySpace will only remove or preserve the profile of a deceased user at the request of the next of kin or the executor of the estate. If you have access to the email account tied to the MySpace profile, you may retrieve the password by going to www.myspace.com/auth/resetpassword. Once you have access, reset the password, and you will be able to access the account. Once in the account, select "report abuse," on the profile you wish to delete or preserve.

Chapter Summary

Make a list of Internet and social media sites: Go through the decedent's internet browser bookmarks and history to determine sites for which she may have had login credentials.

Determine the site's policy: If the site's information was not listed in this chapter, go to the site and select help or contact to inquire about closing the account and releasing the decedent's information.

Contact the site provider: Follow the sites' procedures for closing an account.

☑ ***Actions Steps***

☐ ____________________

☐ ____________________

☐ ____________________

☐ ____________________

☐ ____________________

☐ ____________________

☐ ____________________

☐ ____________________

☐ ____________________

☐ ____________________

☐ ____________________

☐ ____________________

☐ ____________________

☐ ____________________

☐ ____________________

☐ ____________________

☐ ____________________

☐ ____________________

My Notes

Conclusion

The journey you are about to embark on (or have already started) will not be easy. There will surely be moments of frustration, anger, and perhaps disappointment with how the world treats people that have recently lost someone important in their lives. Some of the items addressed in this book need immediate attention. Other tasks can wait until you are ready to deal with them.

It is my hope that this book has been or will be helpful to you and your family. I also want to continually improve future editions of the book for other people who will undoubtedly have a need for this information and advice. To that end, I invite readers to email me directly with personal experiences, tips, or suggestions that I may add, so that we might collectively make life a little easier for people who are dealing with a death.

Please email me at **sphillips@firststepshelp.com** or visit **www.firststepshelp.com**

Best wishes to you as you take your First Steps!

Appendix

Obtaining a Credit Report

This information on the credit reporting agencies may change, but is current as of April 2013. Contact the credit reporting agencies and ask that the decedents file be flagged as "deceased do not issue credit."

Experian
P.O. Box 9701
Allen, TX 75013
(888) 397-3742

Equifax Credit Information Services, Inc.
P.O. Box 740256
Atlanta, GA 30374
(800) 685-1111

TransUnion, LLC
P.O. Box 2000
Chester, PA 19022
(800) 888-421

State Specific Information

Below is a list of state specific websites and phone numbers for: vital statistics, motor vehicles, health insurance, CPA associations, and bar associations.

Alabama

Vital Records	adph.org/vitalrecords/	(334) 206-5300
Department of Motor Vehicles	revenue.alabama.gov/motorvehicle/index.cfm	(334) 242-1170
Health Insurance Continuation	healthinsurance.alabama.gov/ts_cobra.htm	(334) 269-3550
State CPA Board	www.ascpa.org	(334) 834-7650
State Bar Association	www.alabar.org	(334) 269-1515

Alaska

Vital Record	dhss.alaska.gov/dph/VitalStats/Pages/death/default.aspx	(907) 465-3391
Department of Motor Vehicles	doa.alaska.gov/dmv/	(855)-269-5551
Health Insurance Continuation	doa.alaska.gov/drb/alaskaCare/employee/info/cobraPremiums.html	(907) 465-2515
State CPA Board	commerce.alaska.gov/occ/pcpa.cfm	license@alaska.gov
State Bar Association	www.alaskabar.org	(907) 272-7469

Arizona

Vital Record	www.azdhs.gov/vital-records/death-certificate/	(602) 364-1300
Department of Motor Vehicles	www.azdot.gov/MVD/	(800) 251-5866
Health Insurance Continuation	www.id.state.az.us/	(800) 325-2548
State CPA Board	www.azaccountancy.gov	(602) 364-0804
State Bar Association	www.azbar.org	(866) 482-9227

Arkansas

Vital Record	www.healthy.arkansas.gov/programsServices/certificatesVitalRecords/Pages/DeathRecords.aspx	(501) 661-2000
Department of Motor Vehicles	www.dfa.arkansas.gov/offices/motorVehicle/Pages/default.aspx	(501) 682-4692
Department of Insurance	www.insurance.arkansas.gov/consumers/CSDbrochurefiles/Cobra_Booklet.pdf	(501) 371-2640
State CPA Board	www.arkansas.gov/asbpa/	(501) 682-1520
State Bar Association	www.arkbar.com	(501) 375-4606

California

Vital Record	www.cdph.ca.gov/certlic/birthdeathmar/Pages/default.aspx	(916) 558-1784
Department of Motor Vehicles	www.dmv.ca.gov	(800) 777-0133
Department of Insurance	www.dir.ca.gov/dlse	(213) 897-8921
State CPA Board	www.calcpa.org	(800) 922-5272
State Bar Association	www.calbar.ca.gov	(213) 765-1000

Colorado

Vital Record	www.colorado.gov/cs/Satellite/CDPHE-CHEIS/CBON/1251593016787	(303) 692-2200
Department of Motor Vehicles	www.colorado.gov/revenue/dmv	(303) 205-5607
Department of Insurance	www.insurance.ca.gov	(303) 318-8000
State CPA Board	www.cocpa.org	(303) 773-2877
State Bar Association	www.cobar.org	(303) 860-1115

Connecticut

Vital Record	www.ct.gov/dph	(860) 509-7700
Department of Motor Vehicles	www.ct.gov/dmv	(860) 263-5700
Department of Insurance	www.ct.gov/cid	(860) 297-3800
State CPA Board	www.ctcpas.org	(860) 258-0220
State Bar Association	www.ctbar.org	(860) 223-4400

Delaware

Vital Record	www.dhss.delaware.gov/dph/ss/vitalstats.html	(877) 888-0248
Department of Motor Vehicles	www.dmv.de.gov	(302) 434-3200
Department of Insurance	www.delawareinsurance.gov	(302) 739-4251
State CPA Board	www.dscpa.org	(302) 478-7442
State Bar Association	www.dsba.org	(302) 658-5279

Florida

Vital Record	www.doh.state.fl.us/planning_eval/vital_statistics	(904) 359-6900
Department of Motor Vehicles	www.dmvflorida.org	(850) 617-2000
Department of Insurance	www.myfloridacfo.com	(800) 342-2762
State CPA Board	www.ficpa.org	(850) 222-8190
State Bar Association	www.floridabar.org	(850) 561-5600

Georgia

Vital Record	health.state.ga.us/programs/vitalrecords	(404) 679-4701
Department of Motor Vehicles	www.dds.ga.gov/	(404) 657-9300
Department of Insurance	www.inscomm.state.ga.us	(404) 656-2070
State CPA Board	www.gscpa.org	(404) 231-8676
State Bar Association	www.gabar.org	(404) 527-8700

Hawaii

Vital Record	hawaii.gov/health/vital-records/	(808) 586-4533
Department of Motor Vehicles	honolulu.gov/csd/vehicle/mvehicle.htm	(808) 768-4385
Department of Insurance	hawaii.gov/dcca/ins/	(808) 586-2790
State CPA Board	www.hscpa.org	(808) 537-9475
State Bar Association	www.hsba.org	(808) 537-1868

Idaho

Vital Record	healthandwelfare.idaho.gov/?TabId=82	(208) 334-5988
Department of Motor Vehicles	itd.idaho.gov/dmv/	(208) 334-8735
Department of Insurance	www.doi.state.id.us	(208) 334-4250
State CPA Board	www.idcpa.org	(208) 344.6261
State Bar Association	isb.idaho.gov	(208) 334-4500

Illinois

Vital Record	www.idph.state.il.us/vitalrecords	(217) 785-3209
Department of Motor Vehicles	www.cyberdriveillinois.com	Not Listed
Department of Insurance	www.insurance.illinois.gov/HealthInsurance/continueCobra.asp	(217) 782-4515
State CPA Board	www.icpas.org	(800) 993.0407
State Bar Association	www.illbar.org	(217) 525-1760

Indiana

Vital Record	www.in.gov/isdh/	(317) 233-1325
Department of Motor Vehicles	www.in.gov/bmv/	(888) 692-6841
Department of Insurance	www.in.gov/idoi/	(317) 232-2385
State CPA Board	www.incpas.org	(317) 726-5000
State Bar Association	www.inbar.org	(317) 639-5465

Iowa

Vital Record	www.idph.state.ia.us/apl/health_statistics.asp	(515) 281-4944
Department of Motor Vehicles	www.iowadot.gov/mvd/	(800) 532-1121
Department of Insurance	www.iid.state.ia.us	(515) 281-5705
State CPA Board	www.iacpa.org	(515) 223-8161
State Bar Association	www.iowabar.org	(515) 243-3179

Kansas

Vital Record	www.kdheks.gov/vital	(785) 296-1400
Department of Motor Vehicles	www.ksrevenue.org/vehicle.html	(785) 296-3963
Department of Insurance	www.ksinsurance.org	(800) 432-2484
State CPA Board	www.kscpa.org	(785) 272-4366
State Bar Association	www.ksbar.org	(785) 234-5696

Kentucky

Vital Record	chfs.ky.gov/dph/vital	(502) 564-4212
Department of Motor Vehicles	transportation.ky.gov/Driver-Licensing	(502) 564-1257
Department of Insurance	doi.ppr.ky.gov/kentucky/	(800) 595-6053
State CPA Board	www.kycpa.org	(502) 266.5272
State Bar Association	www.kybar.org	(502) 564-3795

Louisiana

Vital Record	vitalrecords.dhh.louisiana.gov	(504) 593-5100
Department of Motor Vehicles	omv.dps.state.la.us	(225) 925-6146
Department of Insurance	www.ldi.state.la.us	(800) 259-5300
State CPA Board	www.lcpa.org	(504) 464-1040
State Bar Association	www.lsba.org	(504) 566-1600

Maine

Vital Record	www.maine.gov/dhhs/mecdc	(207) 287-3181
Department of Motor Vehicles	www.maine.gov/sos/bmv	(207) 624-9000
Department of Insurance	www.maineinsurancereg.org	(207) 624-8475
State CPA Board	www.mecpa.org	(207) 883.6090
State Bar Association	www.mainebar.org	(207) 622-7523

Maryland

Vital Record	vsa.maryland.gov	(410) 764-3036
Department of Motor Vehicles	www.mva.maryland.gov	(410) 768-7000
Department of Insurance	www.mdinsurance.state.md.us	(410) 468-2000
State CPA Board	www.macpa.org	(800) 782.2036
State Bar Association	www.msba.org	(410) 685-7878

Massachusetts

Vital Record	www.mass.gov/dph/rvrs	(617) 740-2600
Department of Motor Vehicles	www.massrmv.com	(857) 368-8000
Department of Insurance	www.mass.gov/doi	(617) 521-7794
State CPA Board	www.mscpaonline.org	(800) 392-6145
State Bar Association	www.massbar.org	(617) 338-0500

Michigan

Vital Record	www.michigan.gov/vitalrecords	(517)-373-3740
Department of Motor Vehicles	www.michigan.gov/sos	(888) 767-6424
Department of Insurance	www.michigan.gov/ofir	(517) 373-0220
State CPA Board	www.michcpa.org	(248) 267-3700
State Bar Association	www.michbar.org	(517) 346-6300

Minnesota

Vital Record	www.health.state.mn.us/divs/chs/osr	(651)201-5000
Department of Motor Vehicles	dps.mn.gov/divisions/dvs	(651) 297-3298
Department of Insurance	www.insurance.mn.gov	(651) 296-4026
State CPA Board	www.mncpa.org	(952) 831-2707
State Bar Association	www.mnbar.org	(612) 333-1183

Mississippi

Vital Record	msdh.ms.gov/msdhsite	(601) 576-7981
Department of Motor Vehicles	www.ms.gov/hp/drivers/license	(601) 987-1287
Department of Insurance	www.doi.state.ms.us/	(800) 562 2957
State CPA Board	www.ms-cpa.org	(601) 856-4244
State Bar Association	www.msbar.org	(601) 948-4471

Missouri

Vital Record	health.mo.gov/data/vitalrecords	(314) 613-3016
Department of Motor Vehicles	dor.mo.gov/drivers	(573) 526-2407
Department of Insurance	www.insurance.state.mo.us	(800) 726-7390
State CPA Board	www.mocpa.org	(314) 997-7966
State Bar Association	www.mobar.org	(573) 635-4128

Montana

Vital Record	dphhs.mt.gov	(406) 444-2685
Department of Motor Vehicles	doj.mt.gov/driving	(406) 444-3933
Department of Insurance	www.csi.mt.gov	(406) 444-2040
State CPA Board	www.mscpa.org	(406) 442-7301
State Bar Association	www.montanabar.org	(406) 442-7660

Nebraska

Vital Record	dhhs.ne.gov/publichealth/pages/vitalrecords.aspx	(402) 471-2871
Department of Motor Vehicles	www.dmv.ne.gov	(402) 471-3861
Department of Insurance	www.doi.nebraska.gov	(402) 471-2201
State CPA Board	www.nescpa.org	(402) 476-8482
State Bar Association	www.nebar.com	(402) 475-7091

Nevada

Vital Record	health.nv.gov/vs.htm	(775) 684-4242
Department of Motor Vehicles	www.dmvnv.com	(775) 684-4368
Department of Insurance	doi.nv.gov	(775) 687-4270
State CPA Board	www.nevadacpa.org	(775) 826.6800
State Bar Association	www.nvbar.org	(702) 382-2200

New Hampshire

Vital Record	sos.nh.gov/vital_records.aspx	(603) 271-4651
Department of Motor Vehicles	www.nh.gov/safety/divisions/dmv	(603) 271-2251
Department of Insurance	www.nh.gov/insurance	(603) 271.2261
State CPA Board	www.nhscpa.org	(603) 622-1999
State Bar Association	www.nhbar.org	(603) 224-6942

New Jersey

Vital Record	www.nj.gov/health/vital	(866) 649-8726
Department of Motor Vehicles	www.nj.gov/mvc	(609) 292-6500
Department of Insurance	www.state.nj.us/dobi/	(609) 292-7272
State CPA Board	www.njscpa.org	(973) 226-4494
State Bar Association	www.njsba.com	(908) 249-5000

New Mexico

Vital Record	vitalrecordsnm.org	(505) 827-0121
Department of Motor Vehicles	www.mvd.newmexico.gov	(888) 683 4636
Department of Insurance	nmprc.state.nm.us/insurance	(505) 827-4601
State CPA Board	www.nmscpa.org	(505) 246-1699
State Bar Association	www.nmbar.org	(505) 797-6000

New York

Vital Record	www.health.ny.gov/vital_records	1-877-854-4481
Department of Motor Vehicles	www.dmv.ny.gov	1-518-474-9981
Department of Insurance	www.dfs.ny.gov	(212) 480-524
State CPA Board	www.nyss**cpa**.org	(212) 719-8300
State Bar Association	www.nysba.org	(518) 463-3200

North Carolina

Vital Record	vitalrecords.nc.gov	919-733-3000
Department of Motor Vehicles	www.ncdot.gov/dmv	(919) 715-7000
Department of Insurance	www.ncdoi.com	(252) 514-4813
State CPA Board	www.ncacpa.org	(919) 469-1040
State Bar Association	www.ncbar.org	(919) 677-0561

North Dakota

Vital Record	ndhealth.gov/vital	(701) 328-2360
Department of Motor Vehicles	www.dot.nd.gov	(701) 328-2500
Department of Insurance	www.nd.gov/ndins	(701) 328.2440
State CPA Board	www.ndscpa.org	(701) 775-7100
State Bar Association	www.sband.org	(701) 255-1404

Ohio

Vital Record	www.odh.ohio.gov/vitalstatistics/vitalmisc/vitalstats.aspx	(614) 466-3543
Department of Motor Vehicles	www.bmv.ohio.gov	(614) 752-7500
Department of Insurance	www.insurance.ohio.gov/	(800) 686-1526
State CPA Board	www.ohioscpa.com	(888) 959-1212
State Bar Association	www.ohiobar.org	(800) 282-6556

Oklahoma

Vital Record	vr.health.ok.gov	(405) 271.4040
Department of Motor Vehicles	www.ok.gov/omvc	(405) 607-8227
Department of Insurance	http://www.ok.gov/oid/	(800) 522-0071
State CPA Board	www.oscpa.com	(405) 841-3800
State Bar Association	www.okbar.org	(405) 416-7000

Oregon

Vital Record	public.health.oregon.gov/PHD	(971) 673-1222
Department of Motor Vehicles	www.oregon.gov/ODOT/DMV	(541) 388-6322
Department of Insurance	www.cbs.state.or.us/external/ins	(503) 947-7980
State CPA Board	www.or**cpa**.org	(503) 641-7200
State Bar Association	www.osbar.org	(503) 620-0222

Pennsylvania

Vital Record	www.health.state.pa.us/vitalrecords	(877) 724-3258
Department of Motor Vehicles	www.dmv.state.pa.us	(800) 932-4600
Department of Insurance	www.insurance.pa.gov	(717) 787-2317
State CPA Board	www.picpa.org	(215) 496-9272
State Bar Association	www.pabar.org	(717) 238-6715

Rhode Island

Vital Record	www.health.ri.gov/records	(401) 222-2811
Department of Motor Vehicles	www.dmv.ri.gov	(401) 462-4368
Department of Insurance	www.dbr.state.ri.us/divisions/insurance	(401) 222-2246
State CPA Board	www.riscpa.org	(401) 454-5780
State Bar Association	www.ribar.com	(401) 421-5740

South Carolina

Vital Record	www.scdhec.gov/administration/vr/	(803) 898-3630
Department of Motor Vehicles	www.scdmvonline.com	(803) 896-5000
Department of Insurance	www.doi.sc.gov	(803) 737-6160
State CPA Board	www.sdcpa.org	(605) 334-3848
State Bar Association	www.scbar.org	(800) 868-2284

South Dakota

Vital Record	doh.sd.gov/VitalRecords	(605) 773-4961
Department of Motor Vehicles	www.state.sd.us/drr2/motorvehicle	(605) 773-3541
Department of Insurance	www.dlr.sd.gov/insurance	(605) 773-3563
State CPA Board	www.sdcpa.org	(605) 334-3848
State Bar Association	www.sdbar.org	(605) 224-7554

Tennessee

Vital Record	health.state.tn.us/vr	(615) 741-1763
Department of Motor Vehicles	www.tn.gov/revenue/vehicle/	(615) 253-0600
Department of Insurance	www.tn.gov/insurance	(615) 741-2218
State CPA Board	www.tscpa.com	(615) 377-3825
State Bar Association	www.tba.org	(615) 383-7421

Texas

Vital Record	www.dshs.state.tx.us/VS/	(512) 972-5400
Department of Motor Vehicles	www.txdmv.gov	(512) 465-3000
Department of Insurance	www.tdi.texas.gov	(512) 463-6169
State CPA Board	www.tscpa.org	(972) 687-8500
State Bar Association	www.texasbar.com	(512) 427-1463

Utah

Vital Record	www.health.utah.gov/vitalrecords	(801) 538-6105
Department of Motor Vehicles	publicsafety.utah.gov/dld	(888) 353.4224
Department of Insurance	insurance.utah.gov	(866) 350-6242
State CPA Board	www.uacpa.org	(801) 466-8022
State Bar Association	www.utahbar.org	(801) 531-9077

Vermont

Vital Record	healthvermont.gov/research/records/obtain_record.aspx	(802) 863-7275
Department of Motor Vehicles	dmv.vermont.gov	(802) 828-2000
Department of Insurance	www.dfr.vermont.gov/insurance	(802) 828-3301
State CPA Board	www.vtcpa.org	(802) 229-4939
State Bar Association	www.vtbar.org	(802) 223-2020

Virginia

Vital Record	www.vdh.state.va.us/vital_records	(804) 662-6200
Department of Motor Vehicles	www.dmv.state.va.us	(804) 497-7100
Department of Insurance	www.scc.virginia.gov/boi	(800) 552-7945
State CPA Board	www.vscpa.com	(804) 270-5344
State Bar Association	www.vsb.org	(804) 775-0500

Washington

Vital Record	www.doh.wa.gov/LicensesPermitsandCertificates/BirthDeathMarriageandDivorce.aspx	(360) 236-4300
Department of Motor Vehicles	www.dol.wa.gov	(360) 902-3900
Department of Insurance	www.insurance.wa.gov	(800) 562-6900
State CPA Board	www.wscpa.org	(425) 644-4800
State Bar Association	www.wsba.org	(206) 443-9722

West Virginia

Vital Record	www.wvdhhr.org/bph/hsc/vital	(304) 558-2931
Department of Motor Vehicles	dmv.wv.gov	(304) 926-3499
Department of Insurance	www.wvinsurance.gov	(304) 558-3386
State CPA Board	www.wvscpa.org/	(304) 342-5461
State Bar Association	www.wvbar.org	(304) 553-7228

Wisconsin

Vital Record	www.dhs.wisconsin.gov/vitalrecords/	(608) 266-1371
Department of Motor Vehicles	www.dot.wisconsin.gov/drivers	(608) 264-7133
Department of Insurance	oci.wi.gov	(608) 266-3585
State CPA Board	www.wicpa.org	(262) 785-0445
State Bar Association	www.wisbar.org	(608) 257-3838

Wyoming

Vital Record	www.health.wyo.gov/rfhd/vital_records	(307) 777-7591
Department of Motor Vehicles	www.dot.state.wy.us/wydot	(307) 777-4800
Department of Insurance	doi.wyo.gov	(307) 777-740
State CPA Board	www.wyo**cpa**.org/	(307) 634-7039
State Bar Association	www.wyomingbar.org	(307) 632-9061

First Steps Worksheet

Decedents Name:________________________________ Relationship______________________

Social Security Number:__________________________ Date of Death:____________________

Professional Advisors

Advisor	Name	Company	Phone	Email
Probate Attorney				
Financial Advisor				
Accountant / CPA				
Realtor				
Decedents Employer				
Banker				

	Legal Documents
❑	Will
❑	Trusts
❑	Birth Certificate
❑	Marriage Certificate
❑	Divorce Papers
❑	Adoption Papers
❑	Military Records
❑	Pre-Marital Agreements
❑	Partnerships or Corporate Agreements
❑	Previous Years Personal Tax Returns
	Asset Documentation
❑	Investment/Brokerage Statements
❑	Life Insurance Policy(s)
❑	Pension Statement
❑	IRA Statement
❑	Bank Statements
❑	Certificates of Deposit
❑	Notes Receivable
❑	Motor Vehicle Titles
❑	Deeds and Deeds or Trust
❑	Health Insurance Documents
❑	Other

Task	Completed
Order Death Certificates	
Death Certificated Received	
Notify Social Security Admin	
File for SSA Benefits	
Locate Will	
Determine Personal Rep	
Will filed with Court	
Employer Notified	
Final Pay Requested	
Final Pay Received	

	Debt and Liability Documentation
❑	Credit Report Review for Debts
❑	Safe Deposit Rental Agreement & Keys
❑	Auto Loan
❑	Mortgage
❑	Credit Cards
❑	Unsecured Debt
❑	Private Notes Payable
❑	Other
❑	Other
❑	Other
❑	Other

First Steps

Debt & Liability Worksheet

Liability Name	*How Debt Held*	*Loan Amount*	*Monthly Payment*	*Creditor Name*	*Creditor Contact*	*Phone Number*	*Email Address*

Asset Worksheet

Asset Name	*How Asset Held*	*Asset Value*	*Loan Against*	*TOD or Beneficiary*	*Where Held*	*Contact Person*	*Phone*

Made in United States
Troutdale, OR
07/01/2023

10926350R00053